NOT JUST
GETTING BY

NOT JUST GETTING BY

The New Era of Flexible Workforce Development

Mary L. Gatta
In Collaboration with Kevin P. McCabe

LEXINGTON BOOKS

A division of
ROWMAN & LITTLEFIELD PUBLISHERS, INC.
Lanham • Boulder • New York • Toronto • Oxford

LEXINGTON BOOKS

A division of Rowman & Littlefield Publishers, Inc.
A wholly owned subsidary of The Rowman & Littlefield Publishing Group, Inc.
4501 Forbes Boulevard, Suite 200
Lanham, MD 20706

PO Box 317
Oxford
OX2 9RU, UK

British Library Cataloguing in Publication Information Available

Library of Congress Cataloging-in-Publication Data

Gatta, Mary Lizabeth, 1972-
   Not just getting by : the new era of flexible workforce development / Mary L.
Gatta, in collaboration with Kevin P. McCabe.
      p.   cm.
   Includes bibliographical references and index.
   ISBN 0–7391–1153–1 (cloth : alk. paper)—
   ISBN 0–7391–1154-X (pbk. : alk. paper)
   1. Occupational training—United States.   2. Occupational training for
women—United States.   3. Poor single mothers—Employment—United States.
4. Working poor—Education—United States.   5. Workplace literacy—United
States.   6. Web-basedinstruction—United States.   7. Open learning—United
States.   8. Work and family—United States.   I. McCabe, Kevin P.   II. Title.
HD5715.2.G375   2005
331.25′92—dc22   2005019589

Printed in the United States of America

♾ ™ The paper used in this publication meets the minimum requirements of
American National Standard for Information Sciences—Permanence of Paper for
Printed Library Materials, ANSI/NISO Z39.48–1992.

This book is dedicated to
My grandmother
Antoinette Ciambrone Grilli
A woman ahead of her time. Taken too soon.

TABLE OF CONTENTS

ACKNOWLEDGEMENTS

All books are true collaborations and this one is no exception. This book truly benefited from the intellectual insights of many individuals.

First I want to thank Kevin McCabe who collaborated with me on this book. What started out as a conversation about providing a brief paragraph or so grew into a much larger and valuable contribution that required significantly more hours than were ever envisioned. Kevin approached this project with passion, commitment, and a great wit and humor that made working together a real pleasure!

Several individuals took time out of their very busy schedules to read through the full manuscript at various stages: Eileen Appelbaum, Cindy Chizmadia, and Mary Murphree. This book is substantially better because of their insights. Special thanks goes to Henry Plotkin who read numerous versions of this manuscript and spent countless hours with us to improve the book and flesh out the arguments.

During the course of writing this book I was fortunate to be a fellow at the Rutgers University Institute for Research on Women's 2004–2005 Seminar. The seminar participants provided intellectual grounding for this work and offered feedback that helped gear the book toward interdisciplinary audiences. Special mention goes to Patricia Roos who has offered me theoretical and practical guidance when I most needed it, not only in the seminar but also throughout my career.

In addition, I want to thank my colleagues at the Center for Women and Work at Rutgers University. They provided support and encouragement throughout the writing of this book. Much appreciation goes to Melissa Callahan, Jeanne Dupree, and Maggie Revuldt for countless hours of transcribing work.

I am greatly indebted to the New Jersey Department of Labor and Workforce Development, the New Jersey State Employment and Training Commission, and the staff of the local Workforce Investment Boards and One-Stop Career Centers. They provided me with access to their facilities and programs, and were always willing to provide information and data for the project. Special mention must be made of Dianne Mills McKay and the New Jersey Council on Gender Parity in Labor and Education. Dianne saw the promise in this project from the beginning and continues to help to ensure women's needs are meet in New Jersey everyday.

I am also especially grateful to the women who participated in the New Jersey pilot program of online learning and agreed to be part of this project. Their time, honesty, and commitment made this book possible, and made the program successful.

I am also thankful to the financial and intellectual support provided by the Alfred P. Sloan Foundation for this project. Our Program Officer, Frank Mayadas, has demonstrated foresight and commitment in moving forward a workforce agenda that provides flexible training options to low-wage workers.

I am grateful for the assistance of the editorial staff at Lexington Press. Jason Hallman and his staff provided immediate feedback and guidance at every step of this project. Moreover, Jason provided support and patience as he took responsibility for the publication of this book.

I am also indebted to the friendship of many who helped shape this work at different stages. Specifically, Fran Benson helped push this book into a larger framework from the beginning. Laurel Brennan helped make light of the trials and tribulations of this process. Nancy Edwards offered daily encouragement, incredible kindness, and much-valued friendship. Johanna Foster has given unfailing support and advice. Asa Hoffman provided assurances that everything would work out as it was intended. Adriana Lentini made me laugh at all the drama. In addition, I would like to thank my parents John and Maria Gatta, who have shared with me the importance of a good education.

Finally I dedicate this book to my maternal grandmother Antoinette Ciambrone Grilli. At a very early age my grandmother had to make the choice between work and education as her family needed her to enter the paid labor force to help financially support her brothers and sisters. As a result, although she had a passion for learning, she never completed her formal education. It is my belief that had policies existed during her lifetime that promoted flexible educational options, she would have not only cherished such an opportunity but also taken full advantage of it. It is to her spirit that I dedicate this book.

SPECIAL ACKNOWLEDGEMENTS FROM KEVIN P. MCCABE

First and foremost I want to acknowledge my parents for the fundamental core values that they instilled in my siblings and me. They have always been the pillars of love, strength, discipline, and understanding. Most important, they taught us that the foundation to a good life was hard work and to take nothing for granted.

Commissioner Albert Kroll, for his persistence and perseverance in ensuring that the New Jersey Department of Labor and Workforce Development was going to reinvent itself into a model for delivering services that would provide for those who need it the most: the unemployed, dislocated, underskilled, and disadvantaged worker. He held true to his principals and he delivered.

Governor James McGreevey, for his leadership and understanding that workforce development needed to be a core priority for the state of New Jersey. He provided the stewardship and the unwavering support needed to ensure that New Jersey would be the national model for rethinking workforce development.

John Heldrich, for having the vision to put forth the reorganization and carrying the torch for its implementation before it was in vogue. He is a true Renaissance man who demonstrated the patience and determination for all those years and without his insight and acumen the reorganization would never had occurred.

To the New Jersey State Legislature for ensuring the overwhelming passage of this landmark piece of legislation. In particular, all the sponsors, especially Senator Wayne Bryant and Assemblywoman Bonnie Watson Coleman.

To the employees of the New Jersey Department of Labor and Workforce Development. They are a group of extremely conscientious, hard working individuals who understand that they can and do contribute to the improvement and well-being on New Jersey's working families. Their assistance was invaluable.

Special recognition to Jody Massimino and Cathy McLaughlin for everything they do to help me exist.

Dr. Mary Gatta, for taking a chance with someone who never had a lick of literary experience. Since we began this endeavor, she has demonstrated a unique belief that we—collectively, as citizens—can be part of the greater good; especially for the individuals who need it the most in society. She is incredibly smart, driven, and shows a passion for what she believes in life. For her, this was not work but a vocation.

PREFACE

In 2001, the U.S. Department of Labor, Women's Bureau, and the U.S. Department of Labor, Employment, and Training Administration, awarded the New Jersey Department of Labor and Workforce Development a grant of $500,000 to pilot a unique workforce program to address the obstacles that single working poor mothers face in traditional educational and skills training settings. They implemented a project to determine whether online learning, which had proved effective in increasing the skills of college-educated workers, could prove equally effective in improving the skills and earnings of low-wage workers. Just under 130 working single mothers, all of whom earned less than 250 percent of the poverty level and whose median income was $18,500, were accepted into the pilot program and received computers, Internet access, and online courses to improve their skills. The goal of this program was to use computer technology to raise these women's skill levels and help them reach higher-level jobs and command higher wages. Upon successful completion of the training program the women were able to keep the computers, thus bringing a computer into homes that, for the most part, were without one.

My task as a researcher on low-wage workers, gender, and workforce development policy was to study this pilot program for the New Jersey Department of Labor and Workforce Development and the Alfred P. Sloan Foundation. My charge was to answer a very straightforward question: *is online learning a viable training option for low-wage workers?* In universities online and distance learning has been used for decades where it has been found to be at least as effective in transmitting skills and educational content as traditional classroom learning.[1] For this project, I was not interested in understanding online learning per se, but instead I focused on determining if online learning is effective for a population that is often excluded from many educational opportunities—low-wage workers and in particular single working poor mothers.

What I did not know when I was approached by the New Jersey Department of Labor and Workforce Development was that this question is really the tip of a huge iceberg that floats within our country's workforce development system. As I delved into this work I began to see the goals of the project as much broader than just determining whether online learning is an effective system for delivering knowledge and skills to different populations. I learned that what is needed are flexible and customized training systems, which allow workers confronted by work and family demands to receive education and job training. In the vernacular of sociologists, we need to "attend" to the lived experiences of workers as we develop and implement workforce policies. This book uses the experiences of the women in this online learning pilot program to better inform workforce development and suggest programs that better serve low-wage populations.

I was intrigued by this project for many reasons. Throughout my college and graduate school training I worked in a series of predominately female low-wage jobs where I met many women who were the sole wage earner for themselves and their children. Several of these women desperately, and often unsuccessfully, attempted to balance work, family, and education. Gloria, a single mother of three daughters, waitressed at night in order to try to complete an associate's degree at the local community college. Stephanie, a recently divorced mother, was trying to complete computer school in the evenings to gain the credentials for a job as an administrative assistant in the office where her sister worked. Not only was she providing childcare to her four-year-old daughter, she also provided eldercare to her father stricken with a brain disease. These women and countless others never finished their educational degrees and programs.[2] They missed their classes when they had to work late, when their babysitter was unavailable, or when they were just too tired to drive to class. The cruel irony is that they knew they needed further education and formalized credentials to support themselves and their children, yet when the demands of life, education, and work conflicted, it had to be their classwork that suffered first.

While the structural barriers that these women faced in completing their education are quite clear, at the time I was unable to suggest a better way for them to finish their schooling. One of the major challenges that they faced was that their work schedules would often conflict with their school schedules. These women were hourly wage earners in restaurants and, quite simply, if they did not go to work, they did not get paid. This is made more challenging as restaurant work has irregular and often unpredictable hours. For example it is quite probable that while the waitress scheduled for the lunch shift may expect to be finished with her work by 4:00 p.m., she may not leave the restaurant until much later. Routinely a waitress's customers could stay at her table for hours, and often she would have to wait for those customers to leave. In fact if she did not wait, she almost always forfeited the tip from that table. At most restaurants servers were earning a base pay of just $2.13 an hour[3] which meant that the tip comprised a significant portion of their income and they were not going to risk losing it.[4]

It was not just work demands that prevented my coworkers from completing their education. Childcare needs also created strains that made it very difficult for them to attend classes regularly. Not only did they have to secure a babysitter (which is not just difficult, but costly), they also had to have contingency plans in place if that babysitter was unable to cover their childcare needs. Without affordable or after hours childcare readily available, their contingency plan was often to skip the class so that they could watch their children themselves. In addition to locating childcare, the mere act of going to class depended on reliable and available transportation. We lived in a suburban Jersey shore town without a very good public transportation system. If a woman's car broke down, she just did not make it to class.

Transportation problems, work schedules, and childcare demands served to create an interlocking system of structural barriers that made it close to impossible for many of the single mothers with whom I worked to complete their education. However I could not provide effective solutions for them at that time. Here I was, a woman finishing her Ph.D., who clearly believed in the importance of education and skills training, yet as a sociologist of gender and work I understood the structural barriers they faced were not going to change overnight, and in fact, would probably be exacerbated over the years.

When I embarked on the New Jersey Department of Labor and Workforce Development online program evaluation almost a decade later I began to see a potential venue for the women with whom I waitressed with many years earlier to better integrate work, family, and education. The Internet is "open" 24 hours a day, seven days a week. The women could take their classes when they could fit them into their schedules. Now, of course, I knew that this would not be a total solution but this initiative provided a new alternative that would at least provide single working mothers with the flexibility to better integrate the competing demands on their time. Here at least was some glimmer of hope.

On a broader scale, this project could bring the issues and challenges that working poor women face in their daily lives to the forefront of policy discussions. What interested me was the degree to which this program vividly illustrated a point made by feminist scholars and activists for years—women face a distinct set of demands from men, due in large part to the unpaid labor they perform. Simply put, women bear the brunt of the domestic responsibilities of the home. As a result of this "second shift"[5] (Hochschild, 1989; 2003), women—no matter what type of education they possess or work they perform—face barriers that are different than men, and are differentially impacted by state and federal policies. Taking those differences into account at the outset of policy formation will help to better tailor policies to individual women's needs. As my program evaluation unfolded, the lives of working poor women, which often are ignored or marginalized at the policy table discussion, took center stage. The relevant question became how could we fit education and skills training into women's lives; *not* how could women fit into education and skills training programs. This question has broad implications as it calls for a reconceptualization of workforce development policy itself in order to attend to the needs of all marginalized workers.

STRUCTURE OF THE BOOK

The chapters that follow offer a journey into the lives of low-wage workers and the public welfare and workforce development policies that are intended to provide support for them, but too often fail. As it stands now workforce and welfare policy that targets the poor cannot effectively address the needs of low-wage workers. One goal of this book is to help policymakers and others understand what needs to be done to help raise the working poor out of poverty. Critical to this is the ability for workers to attain the education and skills training to advance out of entry level jobs, as education and skills training targeted to high-wage, high-demand jobs can help the working poor achieve economic self-sufficiency. To do so I first explore the key components of the debate surrounding education and skills training, focusing on a holistic approach. Second, I examine public policy initiatives that often do not attend to workers' life experiences. I then demonstrate how a public sector initiative of online learning that focuses on the life experiences of women can help deliver education to them effectively. To better understand how to create a more responsive workforce development system that is attendant to the needs of workers and employers, Kevin McCabe (Former New Jersey Commissioner of Labor and Workforce Development) builds on his expertise to share his informed insights on reorganizing workforce development. Finally, McCabe and I engage current public policy discussions to suggest a new workforce development agenda that is both comprehensive and flexible in order to raise low-wage workers and their families out of poverty. What follows is a detailed description of each chapter.

In chapter 1, "A Brief Introduction to Workforce Development Systems," I set the framework for this book. I introduce the concept of the workforce delivery system and the key employment and training legislation that is intended to provide the support and resources for skills advancement. Central to this approach is that workforce development is economic development. Investing in the current and future workforce offers benefits to both workers and employers and strengthens the economy. Such an approach must direct attention and resources to low-wage workers and tie education and training to not only to the local job demand but also to the structural barriers workers experience in their daily lives.

In chapter 2, "The New Workforce Challenge: Finding the Skills to Move Up and Out of Poverty," I focus on the need for education and skills training to help raise the working poor out of low-wage jobs. Critical to this chapter is understanding the current debates surrounding education and training for low-wage workers. I demonstrate that in order for training to provide support for advancement or economic self-sufficiency it alone is not effective and cannot stop at job placement. The workforce challenge is how to prepare workers for the skills demanded by employers, while organizing the workforce development system around the constraints of workers' lives.

In chapter 3, "Workforce Development and Welfare Policy: Explored through an Intersectional Lens," I provide a detailed sociohistorical account of welfare and workforce development policy, specifically focusing on the tenuous assumptions regarding gender, race, and class on which it is grounded. This chapter explores how and why policymakers develop programs or policies that do not adequately recognize or accommodate real workers' needs, but instead advance stereotypical images of the individual who accesses public supports. These stereotypes of low-wage workers are fraught with assumptions on race, class, and gender that make attending to the lived experiences of workers close to impossible. Unpacking these assumptions is central to developing new policies that support and address the needs of workers.

In chapter 4, "Policy and Programs: Single Working Poor Mothers and Online Learning," I chronicle the experiences of the women in the New Jersey online learning pilot program. Drawing on my extensive interviews and focus groups with the participants I explore the ways that the women integrated work, family, and online learning and how they dealt with such issues as technical problems, time management, isolation, learning problems, and childcare. I also explore how access to education helped to increase the women's self-confidence and self-esteem, their ability to be a role model for their children, and increased the overall family technological literacy. The goal of this chapter is to highlight both the challenges that single working poor mothers face in attaining further education and suggest ways for policymakers to attend to these challenges in formulating and implementing policy. This unique case study serves as a model for creating programs to assist the larger pool of the working poor.

In chapter 5, "Rethinking Workforce Development: Reflections of a State Commissioner of Labor," former New Jersey Commissioner of Labor and Workforce Development Kevin P. McCabe focuses on consolidating and reorganizing government policy and bureaucracy so that workforce development is a state priority. Indeed this paradigm shift serves as the catalyst for the implementation of new and innovative pilot programs such as the online learning program. He discusses the genesis of such a reorganization as it occurred in New Jersey, from the initial discussions among New Jersey Department of Labor and Workforce Development officials; to the mobilization of political will; to the extensive planning process; and the passing legislation that institutionalized the reorganization within One-Stop Career System. Critical to this discussion is reorganizing workforce development systems to be more flexible to the needs of workers and the economy.

In chapter 6, "Concluding Remarks: Developing an Agenda for Workforce Development and Low-Wage Workers," McCabe and I present a comprehensive agenda in which we discuss ways to reorganize workforce services in order to most effectively deliver services to low-wage workers. In this chapter we draw upon themes highlighted throughout the book as we maintain that workforce development is economic development that does not end at job placement. We expand the conceptualization of workforce development to include a detailed discussion of *both* educating and reeducating workers. Moreover we discuss ways that collaborations between policy officials and policy researchers can occur and how they can help to create more inclusive and effective policy and programs. Based on this model we suggest how some of the skill challenges of the twenty-first century workplace can be best met by a flexible workforce development system, and can be replicated in multiple locales.

Throughout my work on this project I was reminded of the women I encountered throughout my tenure as a low-wage worker. While many of their names have long left my memory, I saw their struggle in the eyes of the women who participated in New Jersey's online learning pilot project. They all shared a common perspective on life—they wanted better lives for themselves and their families, and they were willing to work hard to get it. The problem was that the system was often not on their side. It is my hope then that this book will offer a new way to think about workforce development that is not only comprehensive and flexible but also takes into account the actual life experiences of all workers in the United States.

NOTES

1. For a comprehensive analysis of the effectiveness of online learning in universities, along with a database of seminal research on this topic, see the Alfred P. Sloan Consortium at www.sloan-c.org.

2. During the time period I worked with these women they had not completed their education. I have not followed their progress since our time working together to determine if they have since finished their schooling.

3. At the time of my waitressing minimum wage for restaurant servers in New Jersey was at $2.13 an hour, legislated according to NJSA 34:11–56 a e t s seq.

4. Of course it is not just in restaurant work where workers lack control over their hours. This is a characteristic of many of the jobs in the service economy. The saleswoman at the department store in the mall is often asked to work additional hours if the store remains very busy after her official shift ends. The receptionist who answers the phones at the call center may have to stay on the job if her replacement is running late or does not show up for work. So if she has a class scheduled after work, it is quite plausible that she will just not be able to physically get there in time, as her work hours can extend beyond her control.

5. Hochschild's (1989) "second shift" refers to the notions that employed women work two shifts—one in the paid labor force and a second shift in the unpaid labor force of the home.

1

A BRIEF INTRODUCTION TO WORKFORCE DEVELOPMENT SYSTEMS

Know that the human meaning of public issues must be revealed by relating them to personal troubles—and to the problems of the individual life

—C. Wright Mills, 1959

Over nine million working families do not earn enough money to economically survive in the United States (Waldron, Roberts, and Reamer, 2004). Collectively these families are referred to as the working poor, and their daily struggles to reach self-sufficiency must be the cornerstone of state and federal policy. For many individuals, even those with the least amount of education and work experience, locating an entry-level job is relatively simple. However the jobs they qualify for rarely offer living wages, health benefits, pensions, or career ladders. Simply working is often not enough. The real challenge for the public sector is how to help advance entry-level workers through the workforce system so that they can reach economic self-sufficiency.

To fully address the needs of the working poor, policy officials must rethink the workforce development systems to respond to the demands of both workers and the economy. This is neither a simple process, nor is it uncontroversial. For decades programs and policies have been set forth that have tried to address the economic opportunities of those in poverty. A common failing of these programs was that they did not attend to the lived experiences of the working poor, and in many cases they are not even equipped to recognize them as a group in need of support. Moreover these programs were often riddled with assumptions of race, class, and gender, and are not structured in ways that promote lifelong self-sufficiency for workers. As a result these workers and their families remain among the ranks of the working poor, struggling to make ends meet.

This book draws upon in-depth interviews and focus group data[1] with the 128 single working poor mothers who participated in the New Jersey Department of Labor and Workforce Development pilot program in order to explore ways to reformulate workforce development policies. I look at the vast material I gathered from a critical perspective—challenging the underlying assumptions within the workforce development system, and I use the data from the program to suggest how we can rethink public policy. This book explores how workforce development policies have ignored the needs of incumbent workers in low-wage jobs (and in particular single working poor mothers) for decades and how these policies need to change. After laying out the problem, I illustrate ways that policy can be shaped to effectively address the needs of this group by providing flexible training options that not only recognize that individuals have work and family demands that may prevent them from attaining further education but also that simply having a job does not ensure that one is self-sufficient. To this purpose I include the voice of former New Jersey Commissioner of Labor and Workforce Development Kevin McCabe,[2] who oversaw the project, as we advance the current thinking of workforce development to reconceptualize how states deliver skills training to marginalized populations of workers. We argue that workforce development policy must be reorganized in order to effectively meet the skills training needs of all workers, by demonstrating—our own collaborative process is the example—the need to bridge the boundaries (both real and perceived) between policy research and policymaking.

The importance of rethinking workforce development cannot be understated. The system of job training and education that currently exists does not adequately prepare individuals to be economically self-sufficient. Skills training is often fragmented, short-term and not always tied to high-wage, high-demand jobs. Even more important is that the existing workforce development system does not address the needs of workers effectively. Job training and education cannot end at job placement. Ways of thinking must be advanced that take into account the needs of these individuals and do so in ways that are able to integrate policy and programs into their lives. To accomplish this we must reformulate how our workforce development system delivers its services to some of its most vulnerable workers.

THE ROLE OF COLLABORATION

Critical to effective workforce development (and indeed all policy) is the spirit of collaboration. There are many forms of collaboration that will be highlighted throughout this book. As noted in the preface the New Jersey project presented opportunities to develop collaborative thinking between policy leaders and policy researchers. As such it seems fitting to begin by briefly highlighting the dynamic ways that social scientists and policy leaders can partner to form collaborations that can serve to formulate, implement, and evaluate policies. Such collaborations have traditionally been viewed with some disdain from both scholars and policymakers. In 2004, the American Sociological Association President, Michael Burawoy highlighted this as he noted:

> Policy sociology focuses on solutions to specific problems defined by clients. The relation between the sociologist and client is often of a contractual character in which expertise is sold for a fee. The sociologist, thereby, cedes independence to the client. All manner of organizations may contract sociological expertise, from business to state, from multilateral organization to the small NGO. What makes this relation instrumental is that the research terrain is not defined by the sociologists. It is defined narrowly in the case of a "client" or broadly in the case of a "patron." (1608)

To my mind such a conceptualization misunderstands the dynamic that can be fostered between researchers and policy leaders and labels the researcher and the client/patron unfairly.[3] The implication is that the social scientist is acquiescing to the desires of the patron; and the policy leader (who is seeking the research) is simply interested in it for its utilitarian value. The static relationship that is portrayed between the social scientist and policy leader does not represent all collaborations.

Instead the researcher and the policymaker can effectively work in tandem, building off each other's expertise. Social scientists, working in collaboration with policy leaders, can provide frameworks that are often absent from typical policy discussions and policy leaders can then advance them at the table. One critical component of C. Wright Mill's conceptualization of the sociological imagination is the interplay between "private troubles" and "public issues"—that is, understanding private troubles within the larger social context. As Mills (1959) noted, one must:

> Know that many personal troubles cannot be solved merely as troubles, but must be understood in terms of public issues—and in terms of the problems of history-making. Know that the human meaning of public issues must be revealed by relating them to personal troubles—and to the problems of the individual life. Know that the problems of social science, when adequately formulated, must include both troubles and issues, both biography and history, and the range of their intricate relations. Within that range the life of the individual and the making of societies occur; and within that range the sociological imagination has its chance to make a difference in the quality of human life in our time. (226)

The sociological imagination is a distinct perspective that social scientists can bring to the policy table. They can bridge the continuum between the individual and the collective by highlighting the role that social structures, social systems, and other distinctively social phenomena play in shaping lives. Social scientists do not just "deliver" their research to policymakers, but instead can actively engage with policymakers. In doing so they help policymakers interpret the findings and directly relate them to practice. As Cernea (1993/1994) noted:

> Social research findings will become effective guidance for future practice only if they result in the formulation and adoption of new or improved policies . . . Social science knowledge must be used not to just evaluate program results but to craft policies. (176)

This type of a symbiotic relationship brings social scientists into a new area in policy work—that of working at all stages of the policy program to shape the thinking, implementation, and evaluation of the work.[4] In addition it provides policymakers with resources and perspectives that may have been previously missing. Such collaborative work opens up new doors within the policy arena and can help to introduce new frameworks to the workforce development field.

WHAT IS A WORKFORCE DEVELOPMENT SYSTEM?

Since the implementation of the 1998 Workforce Investment Act (WIA) the term "workforce development system"[5] has been used ubiquitously but is rarely adequately defined. At its most general sense the workforce investment system "refers to a broad range of employment and training services whose purpose is to enable job seekers, students, and employers to access a wide range of information about jobs, the labor market, careers, education and training organizations, financing options, skill standards, or certification requirements" (Martinson, 1999, 1). Ann Roche (2000) expands this conceptualization by defining three levels of workforce development—a systems level, a level of current workers, and a level of the future workforce. This understanding focuses attention not only on education and training aspects but also on the function of workforce development to address the systems and structures that shape the workforce itself. This is accomplished through venues such as legislation, policy, funding streams, and work supports, which address the need to develop a sufficient pool of skilled workers for the future. These efforts can include worker recruitment strategies, affordable and accessible skills training, and ensuring adequate funding to employ and train public sector staff. Such activities are distinctive from the traditional educational system. As Grubb (1999) notes, "in contrast to the broader goals of education, this [workforce development] system has emphasized occupational preparation, though such preparation may range from broad programs encompassing many occupations to narrowly job—specific or employer specific training" (2).

Of course while workers (current, displaced, and future) are an important focus of workforce development policy, there is also a significant role that is performed by employers. Employers must be partners in identifying skill needs, codeveloping training programs, leveraging public resources, and creating a pipeline for skilled workers to advance. Ideally, this should be a symbiotic association that results in "workforce development [that] is the coordination of school, company, and government policies and programs such that as a collective they enable individuals the opportunity to realize a sustainable livelihood and organizations to achieve exemplary goals consistent with history, culture, and goals of the societal context" (Jacobs 2002, 13). Workforce development then is a programmatic response to social and economic needs that bridges individual workers, employers, and societal needs.

Central to creating a system that meets the needs of workers and employers is the development of a flexible and customized system that addresses the lifelong learning and skills training needs of existing and potential workers in concert with the skills demanded by employers. "In this version workforce development policies no longer address the 'second chance' system as they have in the past, but they are customized to the needs of individuals and employers" (National Governors Association, 2002, 12). In doing so the workforce development system must provide a coherent, easily accessible, and high quality lifelong learning system. This means that all preparation and education for the workplace must be viewed as a continuous process and not an end in and of itself (New Jersey State Employment and Training Commission, 2001). Skill demands are continually evolving and workers need both occupationally specific and flexible skills in order to adapt and thrive. The wide pool of workers in need of these services includes: individuals (typically young adults) who are looking for first-time employment; individuals who are currently employed full or part-time; individuals who are undergoing transitions in their employment (job seekers, the unemployed, and displaced workers); individuals who were employed at one time, but are no longer currently employed (those in prison and retirees); and individuals who have been recruited from other locations for employment (such as guest workers and immigrants) (Jacobs, 2002, 2000).

To sum up then, at its basic the public sector workforce development system is characterized by an understanding that to possess a highly skilled workforce, attention must be paid to the needs of workers and employers. Moreover workforce development must be viewed as an evolving lifelong process that prepares individuals for the changing labor market demands. Yet not only must workforce development address the needs of all workers and employers. To do so effectively states need to take a "demand side approach." The workforce development system, instead of just connecting workers to employers needing their skills, must alternatively determine what are the skills that local employers need and train workers for those jobs (Freeman and Taylor, 2000). This proactive approach broadens the conceptualization of workforce development to include a dual customer focus—that of the worker and that of the employer. This shift emphasizes an important point. The workforce development system must be coordinated with the economic development system. As such "well crafted workforce investment policies and administration can lead to greater efficiencies and result in more effective delivery of services" (New Jersey State Employment and Training Commission, 2001). Simply put, workforce development is economic development.

Unlike many social service programs or income transfer programs, the benefits of workforce development programs are not often immediately evidenced, but instead occur over time. Workforce development invests, at its most basic, in the human capital of individuals. Of course, as with any investment that will pay off in the future it has an element of risk to it. The United States Conference of Mayors in 2002 equated the investment in workforce development programs to the investment that high school seniors make in college. As they note:

> Students enroll in college and incur substantial costs both in terms of tuition, books, and fees as well as forgone earnings . . . However most of the benefits of a college education will occur after college is completed, and the earnings gains will occur over the entire work life. But like all investment activities considerable uncertainty attends the college investment decision because the expected benefits will only occur in the future well after the costs have been incurred and, for some high school graduates, college will prove to be a failed investment . . . Nonetheless, changes in the job content of the American economy have sharply increased the economic returns to a four year college degree. (Harrington and Sum, 2002, 10–11)

Similarly, investing in workforce training for low-wage workers will have economic benefits that are evidenced over their lifetime. The workers may not experience wage increases or promotions immediately upon completion of training programs, but instead may experience them a year or two after it is completed. As such the mindset that guides workforce development policies must be flexible enough to understand that, similar to college education, workforce training programs are focused on enhancing the quality of the labor force and providing individuals with the human capital to improve their lives. Workforce development must be viewed and evaluated as a lifelong process that strengthens workers, business, and the economy.

While this conceptualization of workforce development is comprehensive, still absent is that it must also encompass ways to address the obstacles that individuals face in attaining employment and training services. The lack of access to transportation, childcare, and disability services, along with one's work schedule itself, can make it difficult to attain employment and training services. The workforce development system must encompass a holistic approach that not only provides services but also creates and institutionalizes a structure that is flexible and amenable enough so that all workers can avail themselves of these services. This forces the system itself to reorganize to the needs of workers, especially workers in hard to serve populations, and ensure that their needs are identified and attended to in policies and programs.

WHAT IS THE WORKFORCE INVESTMENT ACT?

To better understand current policy thinking, it is important to briefly explore the seminal piece of Federal Employment and Training legislation—the Workforce Investment Act (WIA). Indeed until recently the public workforce system was viewed within a vacuum with little if any connection to economic development, educational entities, social services, and/or the welfare system. In 1998 WIA, with the institutionalization of One-Stop Career Centers, encouraged collaboration between these systems and structures by suggesting the co-location and integration of services within the workforce system. Most notably, the One-Stop Career Centers were established within local neighborhoods where individuals could access core services and be directly referred to job training, education, and/or other services. Within a One-Stop Career Center both parties—individuals (unemployed and incumbent workers) and employers—have a single location to access. Coupled with a "demand side approach" to training it seems plausible that employers will be matched with workers who possess the skills they need, and workers will be trained for high wage, high demand jobs. To best provide these services WIA is organized around five main goals:[6]

1. Streamlining services through a One-Stop service delivery system involving mandated partners.
2. Providing universal access to all job seekers, workers, and employers.
3. Promoting customer choice through the use of vouchers and consumer report cards on the performance of training providers.
4. Strengthening accountability by implementing stricter and longer term performance measures.
5. Promoting leadership by the business sector on state and local Workforce Investment Boards.

WIA replaced the Job Training Partnership Act (JTPA) of 1982, which was itself a radical realignment of the Comprehensive Employment and Training Act, in response to specific concerns about how workforce services were structured and delivered. There has been a great deal of research explicating the main components of WIA. My goal here is not to engage in an extensive discussion of WIA, but instead to highlight the main tenets of this legislation using the comparative framework suggested by D'Amico and Salzman (2004) to guide the discussion. As they note, prior to WIA, the workforce system was disparate and disorganized. Over 150 separate employment and training programs[7] have operated for decades often independent of each other, making it difficult for anyone to traverse the system. Individuals seeking services did not know which agencies would be able to address their needs, and employers did not have a central location to access potential workers or to share information about the skills their businesses demanded. WIA brought all of these programs under one rubric of the workforce system, with the hope of reducing redundancy and inefficiency.

In addition to a lack of coherence, JTPA participation was limited to those individuals who met a stringent eligibility requirement, as at least 65 percent of clients had to be "hard to serve."[8] This made it difficult to provide resources for upgrading workers' skills, as most resources had to be directed to placing individuals in a job. In contrast, WIA is predicated on the concept of universal access, so that all adults can use WIA services without regard to income eligibility. This provides a venue for the public workforce system to meet a diverse set of workers' needs. That does not mean that hard-to-serve populations are ignored in WIA. Instead there is a three-tiered system so that hard-to-serve populations still have preferential access through WIA's core, intensive, and training services. Core services, the most basic form, include informational resources, self services, job search, and job research assistance. These services are available to all workers, regardless of income, job, or educational level. The next level, intensive services, include short-term assistance to provide individuals job opportunities given their existing skills. The highest level, training services, include on the job training and classroom skills development that lead to a credential and/or occupational specific skills. In order to advance through the tiers it must be demonstrated that one's employment objectives cannot be met at the lower tier.

In addition to delivery inefficiencies D'Amico and Salzman (2004) note that past training systems have also been criticized for not attending sufficiently to the individual needs of workers or employers. JTPA used contract training and that was, at times, based on filling "slots" in programs. Training was often not individualized to the client's career track, educational goals, and/or their local job market. Moreover, JTPA did not actively engage employers or necessarily attended to the local skill needs. WIA legislation addressed both these concerns by providing increased access to workers and by bringing employers into the delivery system as a key partner. This is accomplished through the use of Individualized Training Accounts (ITA) that enable incumbent and dislocated workers to tailor training needs to their educational and career goals. Training funded by ITAs must be tied to skills that are in demanded in the local job market.

WIA legislation established state level Workforce Investment Boards (WIBs) comprised of representatives from business, education, government, labor unions, community-based organizations, and the employment and training services. This represents a significant shift in training policy by divesting authority from the federal government to the state governments. To accomplish training goals the state WIB develops a five-year strategic plan for the state's workforce system, and also designates local service delivery areas where one-stop services will be located. Locally elected officials appoint local WIBs[9] to oversee the local One-Stop Career Centers (Pantazis, 1999).

The heart of WIA is clearly the One-Stop Career System, which was predicated on the intent to reduce government employment and training redundancies, inefficiencies, and fragmentation (Gervey, Gao, and Rizzo, 2004). Critical to the success of this streamlining has been the development and implementation of inter-agency collaboration. The emphasis of the One-Stop Career System to achieve the goals of WIA—an integrated workforce system that meets the employment and training needs of all individuals—makes inter-agency collaboration a necessity (Timmons, Feskso, and Cohen 2004, 19).

THE WORKFORCE INVESTMENT ACT AND THE SPIRIT OF COLLABORATION

It is important to remember that the notion of collaboration among state agencies to more effectively deliver workforce development services and programs is not a new idea. In 1975, Gans and Horton talked about "linking together by various means the services of two or more service providers . . . in a more coordinated and comprehensive manner" (as quoted in Metzel, Foley, and Butterworth 2002, 4). Several models have been advanced to foster collaboration. Two of the most significant are the systems oriented and service oriented approaches (Martinson 1999). Systems oriented models focus on reforming the workforce development system by developing new agencies or restructuring existing agencies. In doing so a systems oriented approach changes the way that state agencies plan and fund programs. Alternatively, a service oriented coordination model unites existing services and service providers without changing agencies or programs funding, responsibilities, or organizational structures. Regardless of the collaborative model that is advanced, the intent is the same: "to achieve a human services goal that cannot be achieved by a single agency, usually due to mission parameters or limited resources" (Metzel, Foley, and Butterworth 2002, 4).

Research on workforce development collaboration among state agencies has demonstrated that the collaborative relationship must become institutionalized within the infrastructure of the workforce development system, thereby allowing organizations to develop distinctive aspects of workforce development programs, such as recruiting, job placement, and post-placement services (Jacobs, 2002; Harrision, 1998). Each of the partners must be willing to work together for the mutual benefit of the customer (be it the worker or the employer). Research has demonstrated that collaboration within the workforce development system can benefit both the state agencies and the clients they are entrusted to serve. Collaboration, Nanette Relave (2000) notes, can open up a broader range of services to clients. In particular she suggests that coordinated welfare and workforce development systems will allow welfare clients to receive employment and training services with other job seekers and not in welfare centered silos; and job seekers can receive greater access to support services. Collaborative efforts also benefit staff as it typically reduces duplicative efforts, provides opportunities for greater access to areas of expertise, and increased communication.

Yet while collaboration is desirable this is clearly not an easy goal to achieve. Several researchers (Timmons, Fesko, and Cohen, 2004; Mazzella, 2000) have highlighted numerous barriers that face such inter-agency collaboration. They find that at the root of these challenges is that agencies that have different roles, histories, cultures, powers (both real and perceived), and priorities are expected to collaborate for one goal. Building on Mazzella (2000) they note that these obstacles include: differences in organizational culture and procedures making risk taking and compromise difficult; funding streams that are inflexible in their guidelines; turf issues in which agencies do not want to relinquish power and/or responsibilities; and differences in each organization's professional training, expectations, responsibilities, commitments, and real and/or perceived power. Further, when referring to the collaborations between welfare and workforce development systems, which are the crux of WIA, several specific challenges arise. Nanette Relave (2000) suggests that while both systems focus on labor force attachment, the "Workfirst"[10] approach of welfare reform differs from the skills development orientation of workforce delivery systems. As such there needs to be clearly identified missions and goals that define the intent of the collaboration. She further notes that balancing the needs of hard-to-serve welfare clients with the needs of other populations can prove challenging as the hard-to-serve population may place more demands on the workforce system. Martinson (1999) also speaks to the specific challenges associated with the collaboration between and coordination of welfare and workforce systems. She notes that these challenges typically are bureaucratic barriers such as differences in performance measures and outcomes (as often employment, training, welfare, and education programs are accountable to various oversight bodies); incompatible management and data collection systems; and a distrust that other agencies can best provide services traditionally designated to certain departments.

WIA tried to alleviate some of these challenges by consolidating workforce programs. Understanding the challenges in reorganizing these programs is critical in the implementation of the workforce delivery system. It is then a goal of this book to bring these needs forward and present a strategic plan to address them through a more collaborative workforce development system. The collaborative structure of WIA provides us with a window of opportunity (Gault, 2002) to offer increased access to education and skills training to the working poor. Most notably WIA allows for universal access to its services. By relieving the strict eligibility requirements, WIA provides a schema that opens to door for everyone in need to access services. This openness brings the working poor into public sector initiatives in ways they have not previously been included. Coupled with using a demand side approach and providing training for high-quality, high-wage, and locally available jobs can help to ensure workers will receive skills that will raise them out of poverty.

THERE IS STILL WORK TO BE DONE

While effective in many important ways WIA has several flaws. First, while WIA encourages collaboration and co-location of services, it still maintains separate performance measures and funding stovepipes. This makes coordination quite difficult to achieve. As such, achieving a real consolidation of workforce services solely within the framework of WIA can fall short of the goal. Second, the three-tiered system often hinders the ability of certain clients to access job training. As noted earlier individuals must pass through core and intensive services before they can access new training on occupational specific skills. While noble in its goal of ensuring that the populations hardest to serve get resources (especially when resources are scarce), this policy has the indirect effect of serving as a barrier to skills training for many members of the working poor. Congressional testimony organized by Wider Opportunities for Women (2003) graphically illustrates this point as they suggest:

> Consider the example of a Vermont woman who sought the help of the One-Stop Center after a long history of employment as a housekeeper. Recently divorced and unable to support her family on her housekeeper wages, she wanted to participate in a skilled trades training program to improve her earnings potential. She was turned away because she had success in the housekeeping field and therefore was not eligible to participate in the training program, which she was told, was for people with no skills and with a long history of unemployment. (5)

Moreover, as will be demonstrated in later chapters, the working poor face many other structural barriers that make completing training difficult. WIA does not fully address ways to institutionalize flexible training options for workers. Changes that better attend to workers' lives must be advanced. What WIA has accomplished is to move these agendas forward and force states to strategically think about how to organize their workforce delivery systems. In that way WIA has been the first major overhaul of the workforce programs in over fifteen years and provides the opportunities for states to make workforce development an economic priority (Ganzglass, Jensen, Ridley, Simon, and Thompson, 2001).

Yet the challenge that still remains is developing programs and models to achieve this goal. Central to this is that programs must be flexible enough so that they both respond to the life needs of workers and the evolving needs of the economy. Flexibility needs to be understood in the broadest sense. The workforce development system needs to be flexible in responding to the skills demanded by local employers and be able to adapt training to those needs. The workforce development system must be able to respond to the needs of a broad array of workers, who may face barriers to training access. One way of accomplishing this is by adopting and adapting new technologies to organize and deliver training. In fact the use of technology is most interesting insofar as it promotes flexibility itself. This provides a new frontier for workforce development programs and policies to embark upon to better deliver services to workers.

WHY ONLINE LEARNING?: FLEXIBILITY AND ACCESS

The New Jersey Department of Labor and Workforce Development, using online learning as the skills delivery mechanism, instituted a program that encapsulated the need to reorganize how states deliver training by addressing issues of flexibility and access. Most notably, while online learning may not be appropriate for everyone—it places a premium on discipline and self-motivation—it had many advantages to both the participants in the skills training program and their families. First, online learning offers flexibility in time and place. Participants can learn at their own pace in their homes (or virtually anywhere), and attend classes when they can fit them into their schedules, taking classes at any hour or any day of the week. Further, online learning is cost effective, as individuals save money and time in childcare and commuting when they receive their training via technology in their homes.

In addition to flexibility in time and space, skills training online offers opportunities for literacy that reach beyond course content. Participants are increasing their skills using the very tool—the computer—that is markedly affecting the skills that are demanded in our labor force. Through online learning individuals also increase their facility with technology and the Internet, learn how to troubleshoot technology, and improve their ability to type. Further, these benefits extend beyond the trainees themselves and also help to increase family literacy. While access to computers and the Internet has increased over the past years, research continues to demonstrate that disparities across social class and educational level persist. According to the National Center for Education Statistics (2002), households with incomes of $75,000 or more are 20 times more likely to have access to the Internet than families with less income. Further, while 63 percent of our nation's classrooms are wired, in schools where 71 percent or more of children are eligible for free or reduced lunches, only 39 percent of classrooms have Internet connections. Alternatively, in schools where less than 11 percent of students qualify for subsidized lunched, 74 percent of classrooms are Internet ready (Van Horn and Schaffner, 2003). As such, providing a computer in the home of working poor families provides opportunities for their children to increase their technological literacy.

The findings of this program demonstrated that we need a new and innovative approach to workforce development policy that includes a comprehensive and flexible agenda of workforce development that can be institutionalized in public sector training systems for low-wage workers. The New Jersey program in online learning for low-wage workers highlighted this change. While this project focused on single working poor mothers the model can be used for other marginalized populations. However, the choice of single working poor mothers for the pilot was strategic. This group exemplifies many of the barriers that low-wage workers face in attaining skills training via public sector initiatives. As noted they face structural barriers including transportation, childcare, and irregular work schedules. These barriers are further highlighted as women bear the burden of the caring labor (Folbe, 2001; Hochschild, 1989; 2003) in the household. Further, gender along with race, class, marital status, and other factors have historically disadvantaged certain groups in regard to public policy. Attention directed to single working poor mothers through this initiative can serve as a model to develop workforce development programs throughout the country that can be directed at many different populations of workers.

POTENTIAL OBSTACLES FOR WOMEN AND ONLINE LEARNING

From the outset it is important to note that while online learning holds the promise of skills training for single working poor mothers, it is by no means infallible. It is important to understand the potential barriers women may face in online learning environments and ways to remedy them. Current estimates indicate that close to 70 percent of students who enter distance learning programs will drop out (either permanently or temporarily) before the course is completed (Furst-Bowe, 2001). While there is very little data on online learning and women, and virtually no research on noncollege women, there are indicators of some of the unique barriers women may face in an online learning environment. I briefly lay out three potential sets of barriers that New Jersey attempted to address prior to enrolling participants in the online programs and suggest policymakers attend to these dimensions in workforce development programs.

Work/Family/Education Integration

Women must find ways to juggle work, family, and educational demands. One way that many women have accomplished this is by adding a "third shift"[11] to their day, and completing their courses late at night while other family members are sleeping. This requires women to be quite resourceful in organizing their time. However, while studies demonstrate that it is critical that adult female learners are more self-motivated and self-disciplined than students in traditional learning environments, this in and of itself is not enough. Both family and work demands compete for the women's attention. Family members can make women feel that they are not fulfilling their family role when they try to further their education (American Association of University Women, 2001). Helping adult female students develop learning schedules, objectives, and time management can alleviate some of these stresses. In addition encouraging workplaces to be flexible in hours and work demands helps women negotiate family, work, and educational responsibilities. Because of the potential barriers that women may face it is important to inform adult female students about the demands of their online learning program prior to their enrollment, and the potential conflicts that may arise. Many studies have found that students report that they were unaware at the outset of the program that online learning programs are very time intensive and require sacrifices.

Technical Problems

The majority of online learners experience some kind of technical problems during their online learning course. Most commonly students report problems with their servers, networks, software, and slow Internet speeds. Therefore, reliable technical support is essential for success in online learning programs. In addition to technical problems that may arise online, online learners should have familiarity with computers. Research has found a real gender gap in regards to comfort level with technology and computers. Female students who may have less experience with technology can become frustrated with distance learning courses that require extensive use of the computer (Bruner, Bennett, and Honey, 1998). In addition, some online students experience "cognitive overload," as they encounter problems navigating the Internet. Since the Internet is a hypermedia environment, routing through it requires an understanding of how to access information online. Specifically, students must know how to navigate online from one place to another, identify and evaluate relevant information and files, save files and web addresses, and relate online information with other sources (Djoudi and Harous, 2001).

Isolation

Adult female students in online learning programs also report that they must work hard to try to prevent feelings of isolation while completing coursework. In fact, the "human" element to the experience of online learning often helps to counter a myriad of problems that students may face. Adult female students report feeling isolated from both the teacher and other students. In a recent study of 40 female online students, 30 percent reported that they did not feel they had significant interaction with the instructor. The students found that it was difficult to maintain their motivation for the course without instructor feedback (Furst-Bowe, 2001). Studies of adult female learners suggest that a great deal of informal discussion often occurs among students via technology (Furst-Bowe, 2001), but students also find it helpful to meet face-to-face with the instructor and other students (Bloomfield, 2001).

While it is critical to be cognizant of these potential obstacles, online learning does provide a new opportunity for working poor single mothers to access education and skills training in a manner that offers them a degree of flexibility and control over their time and responsibilities. However, to best deliver online training to working poor single mothers and the working poor in general, it is necessary to fully understand the socioeconomic context in which they live. Not only is such an analysis absent from most workforce policy discussions, it plays an important role in the actual implementation of online learning for this population. One cannot simply superimpose the organization of current university online learning within the workforce development system. Potential obstacles facing workers as they use online learning technology, and the potential barriers within their work and family structures that could impact their educational participation, must be acknowledged.

While online learning offers opportunities to address some of the challenges that the working poor face in accessing education and skills training, this only represents part of the story. Much debate surrounds job training policy in the United States. I contend that education and skills training are critical to raise the working poor out of poverty, yet this training must be accessible and targeted. In the next chapter I engage the key pieces of the dialogue that explores the role training and education plays in improving individuals' economic self-sufficiency.

NOTES

1. I was provided a great deal of access to the participants in the program by the New Jersey Department of Labor and Workforce Development and was able to collect data on all aspects of the program. I conducted face-to-face interviews

with each of the women at the beginning of the program, and sets of focus groups and phone interviews with the women during their tenure in the program. I then conducted face-to-face and phone interviews with the women as they completed the program. In addition I attended orientations, information sessions, and other meetings of the women during their year in the program and assessed their progress in the courses, job promotions, and changes in their wages.

2. McCabe was in leadership roles at the New Jersey Department of Labor and Workforce Development during the tenure of this pilot program. He served both as the Deputy Commissioner and then Commissioner of the Department from 2002 to 2004.

3. Others have critiqued on this point. See Nielsen (2004).

4. It is important to note that this type of work is not typically valued by academics. As Appaduri (2002, 280) noted, "many U.S. scholars are suspicious of any form of applied or policy driven research."

5. Throughout this book the terms "workforce development system" and "workforce investment system" will be used interchangeably.

6. These goals are taken from summaries written by the Chicago Jobs Council (2003) and Buck (2002).

7. These included programs operating under JTPA, Vocational Rehabilitation, Vocational Education, and Wagner-Peysner, among other entities (D'Amico and Salzman, 2004).

8. Hard to serve refers to individuals who possess at least one barrier to employment, such as physical, mental health, or substance abuse problems; domestic violence, language barriers, and/or lack of education, work experience, or skills.

9. The local WIBs replace the local Private Industry Councils (PICs) that were established under JTPA.

10. "Workfirst" refers to programs that mandate participants to perform paid work as a prerequisite to receiving welfare benefits.

11. This term, coined by the American Association of University Women (AAUW), builds on Hochschild's (1989) idea of the second shift. The third shift of education adds to women's existing shifts of paid and unpaid labor.

2

THE NEW WORKFORCE CHALLENGE: FINDING THE SKILLS TO MOVE UP AND OUT OF POVERTY

Imagine you are a high school educated single mother with two children under the age of ten. You are working two jobs—3 days you are a part-time bookkeeper at your local church, and your weekends are spent waitressing at the diner by your apartment. You earn about $15,000 a year, and are literally living paycheck to paycheck. A few slow shifts at the diner in a week and you are unable to pay all your bills this month. You know you need skills training in order to get a higher paying job, but you do not know when you will fit classes into your day or how you will pay for them. Yet time binds and financial cost are only some of the barriers that you face in trying to attain workplace skills. Locating affordable and "off hours" child-care (such as on nights and weekends when many classes are offered) often proves to be a daunting and expensive task. In addition, you may be among the one-third of families earning $15,000 or less who do not own a car, making the act of just getting to class a challenge. What are you to do?

Throughout the United States this experience is repeated daily as low-wage workers attempt to find ways to integrate work, family, and education in order to improve their lives. Indeed, a considerable number of individuals work full time and still do not earn enough money to attain economic self-sufficiency. The fact that they work for a living and remain unable to care for their families should compel government policymakers to not only recognize them as a group in poverty, but also to formulate new and innovative ways to alleviate their plight. However, for the most part, policymakers have not addressed either of these issues. Our traditional welfare and workforce development policies[1] do not provide the working poor with the adequate social, economic, and/or educational supports that will help them raise themselves and their families out of poverty. Often these policies are not even equipped to recognize working individuals as a group deserving of significant governmental benefits. Only a small portion of federal workforce development policies offer support to incumbent workers. Further, those policies that do offer post-employment supports are often very limited in their scope. Most of these funds are earmarked to aid individuals that are former welfare recipients and dislocated workers, thereby excluding many low-wage workers. Consequently, many of these individuals have never walked into their local welfare office or federally mandated One-Stop Career Center.[2] Moreover, many have never received public supports in the form of food stamps, welfare subsides, or job training.[3] Federal job training programs have enrolled less than 3 percent of the eligible disadvantaged population (Bartik, 2001, 88). This is a nationwide problem, which stems from the fact that very few (if any) agencies or institutions serve low-wage workers as part of their core mission (Miller, Molina, Grossman, and Golanka, 2004). As noted in the previous chapter the three-tiered training system of WIA serves often to exclude the working poor from direct occupational skills training. Such institutional neglect ensures that many low-wage workers remain invisible within our public system of support.

The conceptualization of the working poor in public supports is most directly related to the troubling foundation of welfare reform and workforce development in which the goal of these programs is to place individuals in jobs with the belief that holding any job is "good." It follows from this line of reasoning that if someone is employed we do not need to direct social policies and supports to him/her, as it will be up to the individual to improve his/her economic status. This logic continues to trap many workers "in the Death Valley of the job market, working as janitors and clerks, child-care workers, and nursing home assistants" (Massing 2002, 22) with low wages, job insecurity, and no or very little healthcare coverage.

The question to be addressed is how can we redirect public policy to effectively attend to the needs of the working poor? Of course, when we focus attention on this question, one cannot lose sight of the many citizens who do not have access to jobs in the first place. A reconceptualization of public policy to include the needs of low-wage workers must not occur to the exclusion of others. Yet it is not as simple as just changing eligibility requirements so that the working poor can be included in existing programs. As noted in the previous chapter WIA does offer universal access to training services yet the growth of the working poor still continues to escalate. Instead we must refashion public policies and programs so that they not only include the *working* poor, but also take into account and address the needs and experiences of all individuals. That is, policy should adapt to the worker's needs, not try to fit them into policy and programs.

WHO ARE THE WORKING POOR?

The United States Department of Labor classified 7.4 million workers as members of the working poor,[4] using a strict definition of the working poor to include only individuals who spent at least 27 weeks in the labor force (either working or looking for work), but whose incomes fell below the official poverty line. Many factors contribute to one's likelihood of being among the working poor and these factors can provide clues as to how to design programs to address their needs. To that purpose it is important to briefly highlight key demographic characteristics of the working poor in the United States.

According to the United States Department of Labor, in 2002, about 71 percent of the working poor were white. Yet this does not fully capture the probability that different racial-ethnic groups will be among the working poor. When one looks across racial categories at the proportion of the working poor relative to their population distribution, blacks and Hispanics are twice as likely to be working poor than are whites.[5] In regard to gender overall women have a higher likelihood of being among the working poor than do men (6 percent for women versus 4.7 percent for men). Indeed the proportion of individuals who worked in 2002 but still remained in poverty was higher among women than men across almost all racial-ethnic groups.[6]

Further, the rising prevalence of women as the sole providers for their families contributes to women's increased representation among the working poor. Specifically, women who were never married, divorced, separated, or widowed, and who had children under eighteen years old earned on average significantly less than married women with children under eighteen (median weekly earnings of $430 and $524, respectively) (U.S. DOL, 2002). Single mothers with children under six years old fared the worst, earning a median weekly income of only $379. As a result, families maintained by women with children under eighteen years old have the highest probability of living in poverty—a rate of 21.9 percent. This is more than double the rate of families maintained by men with children under eighteen years old (rate of 10.1 percent) and four times greater than the rate of married couple families with children (rate of 4.9 percent) (U.S. DOL, 2002).

In addition to racial-ethnic and gender differences among the working poor, educational attainment is also a significant factor in predicting one's likelihood of being among the working poor. In 2002 only 1.6 percent of college graduates were considered among the working poor, as compared with 6.1 percent of high school graduates and 14.6 percent of high school dropouts (U.S. DOL, 2002). Of course educational level is inextricability tied to the available job opportunities that one has. Many jobs that do not require higher levels of education typically are characterized by lower earnings, thereby decreasing one's chances of attaining self-sufficiency via employment. For example, service occupations, were 2.2 million of the working poor were employed, accounted for 29 percent of the total working poor in the United States (U.S. DOL, 2002).

It is important to note that the strict definition of the working poor used by the United States Department of Labor excludes a large group of workers and their families who earn above the federal poverty line, but yet do not have enough income to support themselves. The poverty line itself is a problematic measure of self-sufficiency as it is just set too low. In fact since the poverty line was first developed in the 1960s it has only been updated to reflect inflation, and does not capture the myriad of other needs that individuals must have in the twenty-first century.[7] Many assistance programs have recognized the inadequacy of the poverty line and have used a multiple of it to assess need for programs. In the New Jersey online learning project, for example, individuals were eligible for participation if they earned 250 percent or less of the poverty line. This is important as it indicates a more comprehensive understanding of what it takes to reach economic self-sufficiency. Moreover, it also brings attention to the fact that a larger number of workers truly are among the working poor. Using then the guidelines of the New Jersey project, about two-fifths of all U.S. households, and well over half of black and Hispanic households, have family incomes that are below 250 percent of the poverty line ($43,700 in 2001). These households are about evenly split between low income ($\le$ $25,000 a year) and lower middle class (> $25,000 and < $43,700) families, and remain stuck in low-wage work that does not economically provide for themselves and their families.[8]

The demographic composite demonstrates that a confluence of factors including identity (via gender, race-ethnicity, and marital status), educational level, occupation, and the rise of female headed households all influence the likelihood that one will be among the working poor. These factors, along with social structures and economic systems, contribute to the growing numbers of the working poor.

WORKING AND IN POVERTY

U.S. workers clearly face significant workforce challenges in the new post-industrial economy. Indeed, as this country continues to advance into a future of high skill and high wage jobs, many American workers are in danger of being left behind. Political rhetoric surrounding poverty alleviation often presupposes that hard work alone will provide economic success for underprivileged members of our society. Significant portions of our public monies are directed to "Workfirst" programs, with the idea to provide training and other support to just getting someone employed. Yet what this reasoning ignores is that often people will work as hard as they can in entry-level jobs, but will not raise themselves out of poverty. In fact, many low-wage jobs can actually exacerbate poverty, as one's income can exclude them from public subsidies, while simultaneously increasing their expenditures on childcare, transportation, clothing, and other necessary costs that enable their employment. While the socio-historical components of public policy will be considered in the next chapter in greater detail, it is important here to understand how low wages and workplace characteristics can keep workers in poverty. The trajectory into poverty is predicated on the fact that despite employment, individuals may not be able to make ends meet. The economics of this phenomena are based on relatively simple facts— many jobs (including many newly created jobs) do not pay a living wage, and these jobs often do not offer upward mobility into high paying jobs. Interspersed in this discussion is how gender and race play a significant role in compounding the probability of an individual being among the ranks of the working poor.

To start let us focus on wages. Working full time at minimum wage a worker earns approximately $14,000 a year.[9] Yet even that may be an optimistic account of one's income at minimum wage. Many of the jobs in the service sector are paid on commissions or tips. Restaurant servers, attendants (such as those in parking lots or bathrooms), salespeople, and numerous others, all earn less than the $5.15 minimum wage.[10] Instead they can earn as little as $2.13 an hour in many places. The tips they receive are intended to make up the difference and raise the workers earnings to the paltry minimum wage level. Yet this is rarely the case. Tips are not a guaranteed income. Instead they are discretionary income, dependent on the whims of the customer. In fact "like the universal gift, the tip is received for services normally expected, but can never be demanded . . . It cannot be pressed for as an economic right" (Mars and Nicod, 1984, 75). Many low-wage workers then have no right to a significant portion of their income. Further, when we look more closely at the demographics of minimum wage workers, it becomes clear that gender, race-ethnicity, and immigrant status play a significant role. Women disproportionately occupy jobs that are at or slightly above the minimum wage. Data from the 2003 Current Population Survey demonstrate that in the United States 4.5 million women earn between $5.17 and $7.00 an hour, and another 4.7 million women earn between $7.00 and $8.00 an hour. A significant number of these workers (three million) are mothers and 623,000 are single mothers (Appelbaum et al., 2004, 7). When we take immigrant status into account further trends emerge. Thirteen percent of immigrant women and 9 percent of immigrant men earn less than the minimum wage, as compared with 9 percent of native women and 6 percent of native men. Moreover, 40 percent of immigrant women and 36 percent of immigrant men earn slightly above minimum wage, taking home 100 to 200 percent above the $5.15 an hour wage (Capps, et al., 2003). They often work many hours, as four out of ten minimum wage workers hold full-time jobs (Sklar, Mykyta, and Wefald, 2001).

Not only do marginalized groups comprise a large number of the minimum and low-wage workers, they also face a significant factor that decreases their ability to reach self-sufficiency—the wage gap based on gender and race. There is a well documented history clearly demonstrating that men outearn women across all social categories, occupations, and industries (Reskin and Padavic, 2002; Roos and Gatta, 1999). As a result, women experience decreased labor market rewards for the work that they perform. However, it is important to note that the pay gap does not affect all women equally. Reskin and Padavic (1994, 2002), among others, have found that while all women earn less then men in comparable positions, black and Hispanic women face additional costs. Specifically, black women earn approximately 87 percent of white women's wages, while Hispanic women earn about 70 percent of white women's wages (Reskin and

Padavic, 2002, 124–26). The ubiquity of the gender-based pay is a significant contributor to women's poverty, as women are losing critical income as a result of pay discrimination.[11]

Gender impacts wages in other ways. Because women hold a significant portion of the service sector jobs they bear the brunt of the uncertainty in their income. According to the United States Bureau of Labor Statistics, in 2002 women made up 77 percent of apparel salesworkers, 78 percent of cashiers, 73 percent of receptionists, 94 percent of cleaners and servants, 75 percent of waitresses, and 99 percent of family childcare providers. In fact, of the more than 70 million new jobs created in the past four decades, 43 million of them went to women and more than 30 million of them were created in the service sector alone (Johnson, 2002). The stratification of men and women into different occupations, jobs, industries, and sectors is referred to as sex segregation and contributes to women's low wages. Sex segregation is a salient feature of our labor market. The index of occupational segregation, which measures the proportion of women who would have to change occupations (from a predominately female occupation to a male dominated one) to eliminate sex segregation, in 2000 was 52.1. In substantive terms this means that approximately 52 percent or 39 million women would have to change occupations for the labor market not to be segregated (Reskin and Padavic, 2002, 67).

Quite simply, the more segregated the labor market, the more women and men are concentrated in different jobs and occupations and the increased probability of women receiving decreased labor market rewards relative to men. Sex segregation analyses have also been the cornerstone of many institutional explanations of the earnings gap between men and women[12] (Bielby and Baron, 1986; Marini, 1989; Petersen and Morgan, 1995; Roos and Gatta, 1999). Occupations that are predominately female consistently pay less than occupations that are predominately male or mixed-sex (Reskin and Padavic, 2002). This is directly related to the devaluing of women's work. One of the main components of devaluing women's work is the lack of value associated with caregiving, which is conceptualized as a "natural" aspect of being a woman, and not a skill that needs to be financially rewarded. Folbe (2001) has noted that women experience a "care penalty" for working in service sector, healthcare, and other jobs that involve nurturance, caring, and other forms of support labor.

Occupation segregation by race and ethnicity is also an important component of low wages for many groups in the United States. For example in 2000 the leading occupations for black men were truck driver, janitor/

cleaner, salaried manager/administrator, and cook. For Hispanic men the top five occupations in 2000 were truck driver, cook, janitor/cleaner, farm worker, and gardener/groundskeeper. Conversely, the leading occupations white men were employed in 2000 were salaried manager/administrator, salaried sales supervisor, proprietor, truck driver, carpenter, sales representative, mining manufacturing, and wholesale (Padavic and Reskin, 2002). As evident, men of color were more concentrated in low-wage occupations in the services and farming industries than their white male counterparts.

The growth of service sector jobs is not only associated with low wages, but also creates working conditions that make it difficult to advance up the career ladder. Service sector work is notorious for high levels of job insecurity and little (or even no) career promotional opportunities, healthcare coverage, and union protections. Many researchers, including Barbara Ehrenreich (2002) and Randy Albeda and Chris Tilly (1997), have argued that there are no "secret" economies helping supplement the poor, as our conventional wisdom and popular media sometimes suggest. Instead there are actually extra costs that the working poor must pay in order to survive. They must pay weekly or nightly rates at hotels when they cannot secure housing. They must often eat out, since when one is living in their car or hotel room, there is often not a readily available kitchen. And without health insurance they often skips doctor's appointments, often leading to more costly health bills and emergency room visits down the road.

Heather Boushey, Chauna Brocht, Bethney Gundersen, and Jared Bernstein (2001) in their report *Hardships in America: The Real Story of Working Families* quantitatively detail hardships that face families, and counterintuitively perhaps, found that in some cases serious hardships were actually more prevalent among families in which a member worked in the paid labor force as opposed to families that did not have a member performing waged work. For example, "families that do not have a worker were less likely to go without health insurance (22 percent of those families), relative to families with a part-time worker (43 percent of those families) and families with a full-time worker (35 percent of those families)" (35). This finding is directly related to the absence of publicly funded healthcare for the working poor. As the authors aptly note, "Medicaid families are, on average, poorer than families without health insurance at all, since in order to get Medicaid an adult must either be on public assistance or have recently left public assistance for employment. Working poor families are, in most states, left without health insurance coverage, even though they have only marginally higher incomes" (38). The authors find that the correlation between a lack of health insurance and increased hardships is strong, and also a significant predicator of experiencing other hardships. In addition to healthcare hardships, working families also have higher rates of missing or late housing and/or utility payments and food insecurities. A significant conclusion of this study is that while employment is critical, it is not enough for families to escape hardships. Indeed families earning below 200 percent of poverty with a full-time worker still experience serious hardships. The striking finding for my purposes is that underemployed households tend to experience greater hardships than do unemployed and other nonworking households.

It is clear then one can work full time and not raise themselves and their families out of poverty. Moreover, our policies seem to be exacerbating the issue. The 1996 Personal Responsibility and Work Opportunity Act (PROWA), with its five-year lifetime limits and increased work requirements, has helped to accelerate the growing pool of the working poor. Former United States Secretary of Labor Robert Reich has noted "a consequence of welfare reform has been to move several million people from being considered 'undeserving' poor because they did not work, to being viewed as the 'deserving' poor, because they do. Most welfare recipients are as poor as they were before, but the fact that they work for a living has altered the politics surrounding the question of what to do about their 'poverty' (Reich, 2002, xi). Reich points to an important point regarding our social support system. Under welfare reform, welfare rolls dropped 43 percent and welfare reform was heralded as a success. Yet the self-sufficiency level of former welfare recipients was not greatly improved as this group just simply joined the ranks of other low-wage workers. In a study of this shift the Urban Institute (1999) found that those who recently left welfare were experiencing the same low wages and job insecurity as low-income mothers who had not been on welfare. This finding prompted the Urban Institute to conclude "policies to encourage and support work might usefully be focused more generally on low income families with children, rather than directing services specifically to former welfare recipients" (Massing, 2002, 22).

An Upjohn Institute study conducted by Gregory Acs and Pamela Loprest (2004, 5) provides additional credence to this proposition. As they note, "studies of welfare leavers [those leaving welfare during the late 1990s] indicate that working leavers are, for better or worse, entrenched in the low-wage labor market." Further, while access to employer-sponsored benefits varied, less than half of all working welfare leavers had health insurance coverage from their employers, and a very low percentage reported using childcare subsidies. Such evidence continues to demonstrate that although one may be employed, one is not guaranteed a route out of poverty. In fact, Edin and Lein's (1997) study[13] of Aid to Families with Dependent Children[14] recipients found that although the bulk of the recipients could secure jobs, the wages they earned were unable to cover the costs associated with childcare, transportation, housing, work clothes, and other necessities. Employment then does not guarantee self-sufficiency.

THE SKILLS TRAINING CRISIS AND THE ROLE OF EDUCATION

If wages and job structures represent part of the problems, education and skills training represent part of the solution. About half of all workers with low basic skills also have low paying jobs, earning under $7.50 an hour[15] (Lerman and Skidmore 1999, 3). The issues surrounding education and training are somewhat contentious with what appears to be two main tenets in the literature: do we take an individualized approach, encouraging workers to attain more education to improve their lives, or do we focus more on social structures and change the way work is organized and rewarded? The arguments can be conceptualized along a continuum, and it is the integration of both individualistic and structural approaches that will help improve the lives of the working poor. One approach should not be advanced in place of another, but instead they should work in tandem. I suggest that we take the discussion a step further and reorganize the way we conceptualize educational access and attainment for the working poor to take into account their lived experiences. Simply put, as we must reorganize the work world, we must reorganize the workforce development and educational worlds.

While there is strong consensus[16] that job training and education are critical to improve workers' lives, the question of how to strategize the role of job training within the broader socioeconomic and workplace system is highly debatable. Evidence demonstrates that a major factor in explaining low incomes is low skill attainment. A large number of workers do not possess the high-level skills demanded of well-paid workers, and without access to skills training opportunities, these workers will continue to be left behind. Labor market trends indicate that there will be significant growth in jobs that require advanced skills, with slower growth in jobs that require basic or minimal skills throughout the early part of the twenty-first century (Carnevale and Desrochers, 1999). Further, advanced skills are required in all industries, including industries that are not typically associated with high-level skill demands. For example, 60 percent of sales related jobs in the service sector require skills beyond those of a high school graduate (Levenson, Reardon, and Schmidt, 1999). Partly as a result of these changing skill demands[17] throughout the economy high school educated workers, to use New Jersey as an example, have seen their incomes drop 27 percent over the past three decades (New Jersey State Employment and Training Commission, 2001). Indeed, these workers comprise a very large fraction of our workforce. In 2002, 40 percent of all workers—42 percent of employed men and 38 percent of employed women—had a high school degree or less. In absolute numbers this equates to 46 million workers (26 million men and 20 million women)[18] who are experiencing decreased labor market returns for their skills.

Annette Bernhardt, Martina Morrus, Mark Handcock, and Marc Scott's (2001) research, making use of a longitudinal analysis of upward economic mobility of two cohorts of male workers (one entering the labor force in the late 1960s, and a second cohort entering the labor force in the early 1980s), provides evidence for the decreased economic returns for workers with less formal education in the new economy. They found that in the later cohort, those with the least amount of schooling (a high school degree or less), were placed in low-wage jobs at a higher rate relative to the earlier cohort. Indeed their numbers were nearly doubled from the cohort entering the labor market in the 1960s. Workers with some college education also doubled their percentage among the ranks of low-wage workers, relative to the their 1960s counterparts (157). The researchers note that from their data two important conclusions can be drawn. First, because the rate of placement into low-wage jobs was less pronounced at the higher educational levels it is clear that "education served to insulate them against recent trends in wages" (157). Further Bernhardt, et al. found that educational attainment also helped workers to achieve wage growth at critical points in their career tenure—in the early stages of job searching and job changing (93). The second conclusion is that education, while important, cannot solely protect workers from low wages. In their sample some college-educated workers experienced an increase in chronic cycling in low-wage jobs. This suggests that education and training needs to be directly tied to local job demand and flexible enough to adapt to the changing economic context.

Other studies have also found that post-secondary education increases one's earning potential. As summarized in the Institute for Women's Policy Research (IWPR) report, *Working First and Working Poor: The Need for Education and Training Following Welfare Reform* (2001), Thomas Karier's (1998) research found that welfare recipients who earned a bachelor's degree experienced a $2.00 hourly increase in earnings relative to welfare recipients who earned only a high school diploma.[19] Based on studies such as these, state policies have been advanced to provide low-wage workers with access to college education. For example, the Maine Department of Labor instituted a Parents as Scholars program that allows welfare recipients to attend college while still receiving access to all welfare supports.[20] This program has clearly demonstrated how providing education and skills training will raise income levels. Graduates of the program earned a median income of $11.71 an hour, as compared to the $7.15 national median income of former welfare recipients (Maine Equal Justice Partners, 2001; Gault, 2002).

Timothy Bartik (2001) has also demonstrated that formal education is critical to the economic success. He found, using data from the Current Population Survey, that finishing high school raises wages more than 40 percent, cuts employment in half, and cuts the poverty rate by one third. Completing a college education continues to improve wages more than 50 percent, and also cuts both the unemployment and the poverty rate each by another half (88–90). Bartik has noted that the economic return of education reflects in part the acquisition of labor market skills taught in schools, yet often these effects are not equally experienced across social variables, such as race, gender, and social class. Using data from the National Center for Education Statistics, Bartik demonstrates that students in the lowest economic quartiles are significantly less likely to possess a high school or college degree than their wealthier counterparts. The same pattern holds true when we look across racial categories, as blacks and Hispanics are less likely to hold either educational degrees as compared to whites.[21]

While completing secondary and post-secondary education helps to improve individuals' chances of achieving economic self-sufficiency, this picture becomes complicated by the fact that formal education does not always ensure that an individual possesses the labor market skills one needs to succeed. Research using data from the National Adult Literacy Survey, found that 40 percent of workers who possessed a high school diploma or GED tested at literacy levels of two or below (Lerman and Skildmore, 1999). In substantive terms this means that they cannot perform the tasks of writing a letter explaining an error on a credit card statement or using a calculator to determine a 10 percent discount (4). Programs that provide skills training tied to high-wage, high-demand jobs can fill this void left by the inadequate performance by the school system.

The existence of such a network of programs is critical as job training represents an educational venue that can provide bridges to college and can help individuals to increase their earnings. Bartik found that, on average, training programs increased yearly earnings by close to $1,500, and some programs demonstrated positive earnings effects for at least five years after the training had been completed (99–101). Further, an IWPR study (2001) also points to the importance of job training as part of the educational preparedness of low-wage workers. Job training may indeed have greater economic payoffs than basic education attainment for low-wage workers (Strawn and Eichols, 1999). In their study job training resulted in a 43 percent increase in income over three and a half years, yet obtaining a GED resulted in a net economic benefit only if it was coupled with job training targeted to the local labor market.

An impressive study on the effectiveness of targeted job training on wages was conducted by the Aspen Institute. Studying national sector training programs, they found those emphasizing technical skills matched to specific job needs in the local area increased the earnings of participants by 320 percent two years after the training was completed. Prior to training the participants average earnings were $4,669 a year. One year after receiving training the average yearly earnings rose to $12,350, and after the second year following the training the average yearly earning was calculated at $19,601 (Conway and Zandniapour, 2002, as quoted in Dill, Jones-DeWeever, and Schram, 2004). The positive labor market rewards highlighted by this sort of study speaks to the need to directly tie education to jobs and the demand skills needed in the local area.

INVESTING IN SKILLS IS INVESTING IN THE ECONOMY

It is not just enough to offer low-income workers access to training and education. As the previous section demonstrated, training that resulted in increased income and career advancement for workers is tied directly to the occupational skills that are demanded in the local economy. As such many scholars and policy officials frame the discussion of workforce development within the context of economic development strategies. The mantra is that "workforce development is economic development." The National Governors Association (2001) has noted that this rethinking of workforce development has emerged from three significant economic and demographic trends characterizing the labor market. These trends focus on skills shortages and changing skill requirements demanded by employers and encapsulate the demands of the new economy of the twenty-first century.

First, they suggest that the onset of the twenty-first century economy was characterized by a tight labor market that resulted in businesses experiencing immediate skills shortages. This was true across industries. Second, they find that long-term demographic trends indicate that even if the economy weakens, skills shortages will continue to exist. Worker mobility, along with an aging workforce that is not being replenished by comparable numbers of younger cohorts, will slowdown the overall growth rate of the workforce. Third, the National Governors Association notes that the requirements of new and existing jobs will call for advanced skills. They highlight that 70 percent of the new jobs created in 2006 will require at least vocational or post-secondary education (10).

Taken together these trends indicate that as the economy evolves, if the workforce system cannot provide skilled workers to fill labor demands, the United States is in danger of falling behind. Indeed the Working Families Project (2004, 6) warns, "the issues of low-income workers is tied inseparately to larger global factors that are transforming our economy. As the nation grows more diverse and international competition intensifies, jobs are leaving the country and the technological gains demand a more educated and better trained workforce." To remain competitive we must invest in the skills of our workers.

United States Federal Reserve Chairman Alan Greenspan summed up the main components of this problem as he noted, "the earnings gap between highly educated workers and those with fewer skills is a problem caused basically by our skill mix not keeping up with the technology our capital stock requires. It is a structural problem that can be and must be addressed because it is creating an increasing concentration of incomes" (Waldron, et al., 2004, 17). As Greenspan notes, skill shortages hurt workers and the economy as they continue to escalate the divide between the "haves" and the "have nots." Without access to education and skills training segments of the U.S. labor force will not be able to exit the ranks of the poor, as the overall societal income gap continues to widen. The bottom fifth of working families, those families with an average income of $18,700, earn only 5 percent of all the income working families earn. Alternatively, the middle fifth (those earning on average $56,100) earn 16 percent of the overall income, while the top earners (those earning on average $158,100) take home 46 percent of all U.S. income (Waldron, et al., 2004, 9). Moreover, during the 1990s, a time period that was characterized by overall economic prosperity, less than half of low-wage families advanced into the middle class. In fact more similarly situated families made the transition to the middle class during the 1970s than the 1990s (9).

As these data indicate policy officials cannot rely on economic growth to raise workers out of poverty or to strengthen the labor force. Proactive steps need to be taken to supply workers who can meet the demands of high wage, high growth industries. To best accomplish this public officials must ensure that workforce development is demand driven. The workers who will succeed are those who will meet the skill needs of employers, and the employers and industries that will grow state and national economies are the ones that have access to the best trained workers. This requires cooperation between the public and private sectors. Now this is not to suggest that employers should dictate the employment terms of low-wage workers. As Freeman and Taylor (2002, 2) suggest, "any given labor market has a wide range of employers, from worker/family friendly and supportive, to single minded and exploitative. An important role for workforce development entities in demand-driven systems is to seek out and work with the more supportive employers—those that pay decent wages, display good supervisory and other workplace practices, and put employees on a path to earning family-supporting wages and benefits."

THE NEED FOR GOOD JOBS

While the evidence is compelling that education and skills training are critical to raise the working poor out of poverty and strengthen the economy, there is still much debate surrounding the philosophy that the role of government policy is a training and not job provider. Indeed the Cold War shift in employment policy from an emphasis on job creation to skills training is well documented (Lafer, 2002; Worthen, 2004; Weir, 1992). For example, the Works Progress Administration (WPA) in 1935 had as its mandate to create jobs. Training was a secondary goal. More contemporary programs

such as the Job Training Partnership Act (JTPA) and the Workforce Investment Act (WIA) had a combined focus on both employment and training
programs (Worthen, 2004, 77–78). The changing role of the public sector
in regard to these initiatives has been criticized by researchers such as Beth
Schulman (2003) who argues that even with more education and training
there are just fewer good jobs to move into. She suggests that economic
forecasts predict that the low-wage market will continue to grow, with a
great deal of growth in labor intensive service industries. For example, she
notes there will be 1.8 million new engineers and software specialists, and
3.8 million new cashier jobs by the end of the current decade. Based on
these predictions several researchers and policy advocates suggest that job
training itself is not a solution to poverty.

Gordon Lafer has arguably been among the most vocal critics in the shift
in policy toward job training over the past decades. In his book, *The Job
Training Charade*, he suggests that the emphasis on training as a solution
to unemployment, underemployment, and poverty was a failed policy from
the start that he believed "everyone knew would not work." Lafer (2002, 3)
posits that policy solely focused on education and training is based on three
assumptions. First, not only does it presuppose that there will there be an
ample supply of decently paying jobs, but second, that the earnings are primarily based on the skills that the workers bring, and third, that poverty
and its solutions are unrelated to sociopolitical structures of race, gender,
age, unionization, and other key variables. Lafer is accurate in unpacking
much of the problematic logic underlying workforce development and welfare policy. Job training cannot occur simply for training's sake but instead
needs to be tied directly to high-wage jobs that are available in local labor
markets. Further, I suggest that when high-paying jobs are not locally available, government policy should play a role in job creation by tying workforce development to economic development and engaging the private
sector into the workforce development plans of the local area. In addition,
Lafer's contention that skill attainment and education itself does not ensure
self-sufficiency is quite problematic. As noted earlier in this chapter, for
example, while the pay gap (be it across gender, race, age, and numerous
other variables) significantly impacts the potential earnings of several
groups of workers, the human capital one brings to a job via education and
skills can positively impact earnings across social groups.

Despite the critiques of the current model I do not suggest that one
must abandon or even diminish education and training. Instead we need to
reformulate workforce development in order for education and training to

provide real economic benefits to low-wage workers, while at the same time address the full spectrum of inequitable structures that impact low-wage workers lives including housing, childcare, low wages, and healthcare. Thus education and training can be seen as an essential part of an overall work-force development system to raise individuals out of poverty. Marcia Bok (2004) has expanded on this paradigm as she notes that, "if access to educa-tion and vocational training [for low-wage women] could improve, it would, in fact, create some degree of structural change as more low-income women of color penetrated the ranks of higher income workers. This argu-ment simply acknowledges that change can require more than one strategy and occur in more than one direction at the same time" (41).

There is then the need to challenge some of the basic assumptions of workforce development. Many training programs are short-term, inexpen-sive, and have not produced high-level results. They place people into low-wage jobs, and the success of the program is measured solely on that place-ment. From the Comprehensive Employment and Training Act (CETA) to JTPA to WIA training time, along with economic support, decreases and then virtually disappears from the moment of hiring.[22] Lafer (2002) further notes there has been a steady decline in federal training resources: "From the peak of CETA activity under the Carter administration to the inception of JTPA, job training resources measured in real dollars were cut by 80 percent" (97). Further, he notes that under the Workforce Investment Act (WIA) training classes have been made entirely optional.

Additionally, WIA funding is tied to performance measures that make directing resources to low-wage workers seem unproductive. "Some of these measures—namely, newly entered employment levels and earnings gains—provide disincentives to serving individuals who are already working and instead face the unemployed or other groups" (Miller, Molina, Gross-man, and Golanka, 13, 2004). Indeed as Carnevele (1999, 43) has sug-gested, while Workfirst policies have met the business needs by providing the immediate mobilization of groups of people to work, they do not address the next step. The jobs that short-term training prepares for often do not provide venues for further education. Bok (2004, 46) takes this dis-cussion further as she notes, "optimal goals are often not achieved because there is a lack of continuity and coordination among basic skills training, occupational skills training, and the need for a seamless training, educa-tional, and employment system."

What is needed is a reconceptualization of workforce development pol-icy that promotes lifelong learning to low-wage workers in a way that

attends to their life experiences and needs. Focusing on training for training sake is ineffective, and indeed many of the available entry-level job
placements do not even require training. Even more problematic is that
once individuals are placed in a job, the public sector training system typically washes their hands of them. Workforce development must provide
supports after that entry-level job, and skills training is a critical part of
that.[23] In fact, in order to achieve economic success in the twenty-first century, it is clear that one must broadly define education and training to
include not just completing a high school diploma or a community college
degree, but also mastering additional training and certifications in technical
areas, information technology, and/or soft skills, and directly tie these skills
to demand jobs in local labor markets. The question then is not only how
to accomplish this for low-wage workers but also how to tie it to better jobs
and provide additional supports that allow workers to accomplish the
demands of work, family, and education. The reality is that much of past
and current workforce development policy is structured in such a way as to
not provide the support that the working poor, and in particular single
working poor mothers, need to combine work, family, and education. In
the next chapter I explore the sociohistorical foundation of welfare and
workforce development policy focusing on race, class, and gender dimensions in order to better understand not only the challenges women face
in attaining education and securing better paying jobs but also to begin to
reconceptualize workforce development policy to take workers and their
lives into account.

NOTES

1. For my purposes in this book I explore the seminal pieces of legislation that
are encapsulated under U.S. welfare reform and workforce development policy. As
will be demonstrated, throughout the twentieth century there has been a clear shift
from "welfare" entitlement solution to a "work" solution (Noyes and Smith, 2004)
to poverty. This shift indicates the necessity of examining both aspects of poverty
policy.

2. As explained in the previous chapter One-Stop Career Centers are mandated by the Federal Workforce Investment Act to be a local office where individuals can receive information and resources on employment and training
opportunities, along with federal and state benefit information.

3. While many of the women in my study did not previously receive public

assistance to assist with training, they did qualify for the Earned Income Tax Credit and Child Tax Credits.

4. Alice O'Connor (2000) has noted that the terminology of working poor is problematic because it creates the artificial distinction between the deserving poor (those that are employed) and the undeserving poor (those that are on welfare). Such a conceptualization ignores the fact that those on welfare do work in both the paid and unpaid labor force.

5. The poverty rate among working blacks in 2002 was 10.5 percent, among Hispanics was 10.4 percent, and among whites was 4.5 percent (U.S. DOL, 2004).

6. The exception was Asian where the rates for men and women were the same.

7. While a full discussion of the poverty line is beyond the scope of this work I direct interested readers to Pierce and Brooks, 2002, for a comprehensive overview.

8. Data from the Center for Economic and Policy Research, CEPR ORG Extract Version 0.9; and is limited to workers aged 25 to 64.

9. Full-time minimum wage in 2002 was $5.15 an hour. This yearly earnings figure includes the net effects of the Earned Income Tax Credit and the subtraction of taxes (Pierce, 2002).

10. This is the federally mandated minimum wage. Some states have instituted higher minimum wages.

11. For a full summary of the gender based pay gap see Roos and Gatta, 1999.

12. It is important to note that there is literature that has begun to question the relationship between sex segregation and the pay gap. Leslie McCall (2001) found such trends within the U.S. labor market. Amassing 1990 census data from over 500 U.S. labor markets, McCall also found that occupational sex segregation and wage discrimination do not necessarily coexist. Focusing on variability across labor markets in flexible/insecure employment, immigration, casualization, technology and trade, and changes in the industrial structures, she found that labor market factors can affect both occupational segregation and the earnings gap differently. There are labor markets in the United States, such as high technology manufacturing regions, in which the traditional assumption of high occupational segregation and a high wage gap hold true. However, McCall also found that there are regional labor markets in which a decrease in occupational segregation did not reduce the sex wage gap; similarly, she also found markets where there were low wage gaps and high levels of segregation.

13. Edin and Lein (1997) conducted their study pre-welfare reform of 1996.

14. Aid to Families with Dependent Children was the welfare legislation before the implementation of Temporary Aid to Needy Families in 1996.

15. This figure is measured in 1997 dollars.

16. Of late there has been research criticizing the job training programs in the United States. Vocal opponents, such as Gorden Lafer (2001), have called for an

abandonment of such programs. While I agree with some of his critiques of the programs, I disagree with his call to dismantle such programs completely.

17. Other reasons include a decrease in the value of the minimum wage and a decline in the manufacturing sector.

18. Data from the Center for Economic and Policy Research, CEPR ORG Extract Version 0.9; and is limited to workers aged 25 to 64.

19. The National Center for Education Statistics (2000) provided further evidence for the "education premium" as women with a college education continued to outpace their high school counterparts (Bae, et al., 2000).

20. Because the program is funded by state dollars, the time spent in the program does not count against the recipients federal five-year lifetime limit on receiving support that was instituted under 1996 welfare reform.

21. Specifically, while 9 percent of students whose families were in the lowest socioeconomic quartile did not possess a high school diploma, only 1 percent of students whose families were in the high quartile did not possess a high school degree. Conversely, while 51 percent of students in the high quartile had a bachelor's degree or higher, only 7 percent of students in the low quartile had the same. Across race, he found that 5 percent of whites did not hold a high school diploma, while 7 percent of blacks and 12 percent of Hispanics were in a similar situation. When looking at bachelor's degrees or higher he found that 27 percent of whites, 12 percent of blacks, and 10 percent of Hispanics hold at least a college graduate.

22. Michael Massing (2002, 30) provides additional credence to this finding through his work on welfare reform. He notes that pre-employment courses rarely have long-term effects. "Instead training and guidance must continue long after the individual enters the workplace. Exactly how to provide this, though, has long eluded policymakers."

23. In addition to increased access to skills training, it is critical to examine the structure of many low-wage jobs in order to help create career ladders within these jobs. Education in and of itself is not enough. The public sector needs to work with employers to create opportunities for trained workers.

3

WORKFORCE DEVELOPMENT AND WELFARE POLICY: EXPLORED THROUGH AN INTERSECTIONAL LENS

Gender, race, class, age, educational levels, among other variables, alter the effectiveness of public policies. These factors play a strikingly significant role in the development of economic and social opportunities for the working poor. Quite often when state and federal governments develop policies to raise individuals out of poverty, there is an underlying social agenda regarding certain groups in this discourse. To best understand this agenda one must look historically using an intersectional approach in order to examine how gender, race, class, and marital status influence the experiences of workers in regard to job training policy. Indeed, welfare reform has been heralded as a success in some circles precisely because it has moved women, and in particular single mothers of color, into paid work. June O'Neill and Anne Hill (2002) report that women have actually "gained ground" as a result of welfare reform in 1996, by noting that there were tremendous employment gains for single mothers post-welfare reform. They report that by 2000 there was a 40 percent increase in the work participation of single mothers who were high school dropouts; an 83 percent increase in work participation among African American single mothers; and the gains for Hispanic single mothers were similar, rising from 47 percent in 1992 to 63 percent in 2000.

Of course what is absent from this analysis is that despite employment women still comprise a significant portion of the poor, as compared to men. As noted earlier, in 2002 the poverty rate for men was 4.7, while the comparable rate for women was 6.0. Yet not all women share an equal probability of being among the ranks of the working poor. The poverty rate of working African American women was 11.8 and the poverty rate of working Hispanic women was 10.0, compared to a poverty rate of 4.4 for working white women (U.S. DOL, 2004). How then does one reconcile the notion that despite such employment gains women, in particular women of color and single mothers, continue to comprise a significant portion of the working poor? The answer resonates in assumptions about gender that have deep roots in the historical treatment of women that originate from the complicated nexus of gender, race, and class that are encapsulated in public policy.

To begin to unpack these assumptions and beliefs it is important to interrogate two bases of U.S. welfare and workforce development policy. First, a great number of welfare and workforce development policies are based on conceptualizations of gender, socioeconomic class, and race that deem certain groups of individuals "deserving" of support and other groups as "undeserving." These distinctions have simultaneously stigmatized working poor single mothers (and in particular single mothers of color) within the public assistance system as both undeserving of social supports and also abusers of those same supports. Second, coupled with these gendered and racialized notions of support is the belief that the goal of welfare and workforce development programs is simply to get a recipient employed. As such any job is thus considered a "good" job, regardless of wages earned and benefits acquired. Federal and state performance is evaluated by the number of job placements that are achieved, and not the quality of the job that individuals are being placed or the skills and education workers will need for success in the labor market. This then casts a large number of low-skilled women in low-wage entry-level jobs without the education, resources, and tools to advance out of those jobs. Indeed, I demonstrate how the gendered and racialized framework of welfare and workforce development policy has deprived women, and particularly women of color, the opportunity to attain education and skills training to improve their lives and attain economic self-sufficiency.

USING AN INTERSECTIONAL LENS

Women's chances of escaping poverty are affected by, and perhaps more aptly hindered by, welfare and workforce development policies. Looking at the contentious and often discriminatory history of welfare and workforce development highlights how working poor women, and more specifically single mothers, have been conceptualized and stigmatized by U.S. public assistance policies. To understand the effects of policy over time on the lives of the working poor, I employ a framework of intersectionality. Such an approach is rooted in the work of scholars studying women of color (collectively referred to as multicultural feminism, multiracial feminism, or postcolonial feminism).[1] Emerging from black feminist theory, scholars using intersectional approaches argue that both race and gender shape women's lives, but neither theory addresses their experiences of race and gender as "simultaneous and linked social identities" (Browne and Misra, 2003; hook, 1989; Glenn, 1999). As such Patricia Hill Collins (1999) defines the matrix of domination, which forms interlocking systems of race, class, and gender. Within the matrix of domination one can be simultaneously disadvantaged and privileged through the combined statuses of gender, race, and class. As such, an intersectional analysis does not just add variables together, but instead explores how these identities are interwoven in beliefs and practices. "Examining the plight of the poor through an intersectional lens emphasizes the contemporary outcomes of historical structural patterns that have resulted in the overrepresentation of people of color and women, especially women of color, among the poor" (Dill, et al., 2004, 1).

Using such a framework one must examine how welfare and workforce development policies themselves are formulated and implemented in order to understand how working poor women are caught in a system in which they are not only unable to support themselves but also unable to acquire human capital resources to attain self-sufficiency via the traditional mechanisms of education and skills training. Indeed, this is the double-edged sword that working poor women face—how do they economically survive day by day and then how do they attain the skills that will enable them to be more marketable for the future. However, to fully understand the current situation it is necessary to trace how we got to where we are. Indeed, it is through understanding the social history of public assistance that we can explore new and innovative ways to provide access to economic and educational opportunities that are informed by gender and race and not based on ideological gendered and racialized beliefs. To accomplish this I draw on the work of numerous scholars to explore why public programs often ignore working poor women even though they are not surviving economically. Critical to accomplishing this is unpacking the notion of social support on which many public programs are predicated. In doing so I focus on the social structures of gender, race, and marital status to make visible how beliefs about these structures are embedded within our public policy and form an ideological underpinning that negatively affects many women's present and future economic statuses. Indeed, it is understanding how the structures of gender, race, class, and marital status both affect the opportunities available to women and their families, and also shape the policies that are assumed to provide them with a "safety net" that we can then rethink and redevelop these workforce policies to better attend to the current and future needs of working poor single mothers.

GENDER AND WELFARE: IT AFFECTS ALL WOMEN

Scholars have conducted extensive research illustrating the gendered and racialized assumptions embedded within the U.S. welfare system. Mimi Abramovitz (2000) has demonstrated that this past century's constant drive to "reform" welfare has less to do with improving welfare and more to do with attacking the poor, and in particular, poor women. An implicit mechanism used in this assault is conceptualizing welfare programs as the root cause of the poor's problems, and ignoring the impact of larger social structures such as the labor market, discrimination, and access to affordable healthcare and housing that better explain the reasons for poverty (Cororan, Danziger, Kalil, and Seifeldt, 2000). This assault, wrought with contradictions about gender, race, and class, has become so mainstreamed that it remains unchallenged in many policy circles. Two of the most significant contradictions revolve around the contentious concepts of "dependency" and "deservingness" (Mink, 1999; Solinger, 1998; Albeda and Tilly, 1997). The definitions of these terms shift throughout different historical time periods and are directly affected by how welfare policy has divided women based on race, class, and marital status. So, for example, while women's dependency on welfare is seen as problematic, other forms of dependency (such as on a husband) are glorified within our society (Albeda and Tilly, 1997). In addition, some types of women, in particular widowed middle-class white mothers, are considered "deserving" of support while other women, specifically single poor mothers of color, are considered "undeserving" of the same support.

Unpacking these contradictions and exposing their sociological basis is critical to understanding how these policies affect women's economic opportunities. Indeed the ideological underpinnings of welfare reform, in appealing to the visceral responses of many white middle-class individuals, are able to mask their inherent social construction[2] and discriminatory basis. This was reinforced by politicians and the media who painted welfare recipients as "queens," "lazy parasites," "pigs at the trough," and always black (Boris, 1998, 39). An intersectional sociohistorical account of welfare and workforce development is necessary to identify the ways that the conceptualization of which groups deserve and receive social supports and which groups do not is actually riddled with semantic distinctions. As a result a white middle-class single mother collecting Social Security payments to help support her and her children after the death of her husband is not considered on welfare, while a poor black single mother collecting Temporary Aid to Needy Families (TANF) is pegged a welfare recipient. Moreover, such a binary conceptualization of welfare is able to obfuscate the role of public policy to provide education and skills training, and instead directs one's attention to the "system" itself. In doing so this enables middle-class recipients of social support to distance themselves from poor welfare recipients.

To further highlight this distinction every semester in my Labor Studies classes I conduct a quasi-experiment with my students in which I ask them how many of them are currently collecting welfare. Each semester maybe one or two students raise their hands. Then I ask them how many of them are receiving some type of tuition support, be it a Pell Grant, low-interest loan, or other state/federal monies. Over three quarters of the hands in the class shoot up. I tell them "congratulations you are all on some sort of social welfare." While many of the students express shock and dismay, some of them do get the message and arrive at a more nuance, understanding of social support. Very few of us would ever question the "deservingness" of educational support, but then we typically do not view it as welfare. Yet when a single mother collects Childcare Vouchers many people automatically bemoan her for "living off the system."

Why is it then that one form of educational support is interpreted as more "deserving" than another? The labeling of the type of individuals who collects welfare and those who do not helps to perpetuate myths about social systems. Perhaps no piece of scholarship so succinctly demonstrates this contradiction as Abramovitz's 2001 article,[3] "Everyone Is Still on Welfare." In this work Abramovitz clearly demonstrates that while conventional wisdom purports that welfare payments overwhelmingly go to the poor, the data demonstrate that social welfare programs serving the middle and upper classes receive more funding, pay higher benefits, and face fewer budget cuts. For example, Abramovitz notes that in 2000 while the U.S. government spent $253.9 billion for means tested public assistance programs that served the poor, they also spent $793.9 billion on non-means tested programs (299). These programs have more elastic eligibility requirements and are able to serve the nonpoor. They include social security pensions, rent supplements, and subsidized public education. Moreover, social welfare is just one form of support that is distributed by the U.S. government. Indeed, she notes that fiscal welfare (providing income supports indirectly through tax exemptions, deductions, and credits); occupational welfare (benefits tied to work including cost of living raises, private pensions, and on-site childcare); and corporate welfare (tax breaks, tax deferrals, low interest loans, tax-free enterprise zones) all comprise our welfare state.

Abramovitz argues that although "nearly everyone is on welfare, everyone does not seem to know it" (306). She notes that instead the visible face of welfare—programs for the poor—are highlighted while the other forms of welfare operate in the shadows. It is this "shadow" location that shields the upper and middle classes from conceptualizing their benefits as social welfare at all. Similarly, very few people questioned the need to provide widows from the September 11 terrorist attacks in New York City, Washington D.C., and Pennsylvania with compensation for their lost husbands' wages after their death, yet we scorn poor single mothers for receiving similar compensation when their partners are absent. The ideas behind both types of payments are the same—that women without men's wages would be in poverty, so therefore the government should step in to assist them. Yet as long as only social support that is directed to poor women and women of color is considered welfare and then further are stigmatized as a negative "dependency," Congress will continue to focus on "ending welfare as we know it."[4] With this mindset in place little attention is then paid to the fact that it is not welfare that is making single mothers poor, it is instead a lack of living wage jobs and social support, such as childcare, transportation, and affordable housing that will allow them to maintain employment and attain the education and skills training to further advance in employment.

This more nuanced analysis of welfare and workforce development has been advanced by several writers, most notably Gwendolyn Mink. Mink (1999) suggests that gender scholars must refocus their questions surrounding welfare to not just "confine our scholarly debates and inquiries to whether and how welfare had subordinated women . . . No one [during welfare reform] was asking 'what should welfare be for women?' or 'How might welfare work for women?'" (185). In doing so Mink argues for scholars and policymakers to not see welfare in opposition to women's equality, but instead should "defend welfare as an element of social justice" (185). Welfare must then not be solely interpreted from the white middle-class perspective, but instead recognize that gender is a diverse category with many prerequisites for equality (188). Kittay (1998) offers a venue to achieve this by reclaiming the term "doula" (which translates to one who cares for the mother as the mother cares for the child) within the welfare dialogue. She suggests that "doulia" (the practice of doula) be institutionalized in social supports by providing assistance to paid and unpaid caregivers. That is, provide support to those who become needy by virtue of caring for those in need (204). Such reasoning in policy appears similar to the family allowance systems, which in conjunction with other public subsidies (such as healthcare and childcare) helped to reduce poverty in many European countries (Folbe, 2001). Such an understanding then would value all forms of caring labor—paid and unpaid—that women perform directly in the policy that is intended to keep them out of poverty.

This is critical as welfare policies define the value of all women and all women's work in a society. Randy Albeda and Chris Tilly (1997, 12) have shown that welfare defines for all of us how low women can go in our economy, as the level of welfare payments and the regulations and eligibility requirements determine the "safety net" for all women. And, more often than not, this safety net is unable to actually function as a support. It is evident that while the self-sufficiency[5] level for a single mother with two children in suburban Monmouth County[6] in New Jersey in 2002 was calculated (conservatively) at $47,881, the most public support via welfare and food stamps she may have been eligible for hovered around $9,360 (Pierce and Brooks, 2002). How then is she expected to attain self-sufficiency, especially as we know that three out of five minimum wage workers are women, earning approximately $14,504 a year,[7] which is significantly less than self-sufficiency. This large discrepancy indicates that there is a lack of social value on ensuring that women are independent economic providers who do not need to rely on men for financial support. Again we return to this conflicting notion of "dependency," quite simply, a woman should not be turning to the state to supplement her income (or even her employer to raise her wages), she needs to look toward the father of her children. And if he is not available or unable she should look toward another man. Indeed despite the fact that this is highly sexist and heterosexist, this belief is actually codified within federal workforce policy as George W. Bush's administration allocated over $1.5 billion toward "marriage awareness and education" for women on welfare (IWPR, 2002, 1). Indeed, as Sharon Hays (2003) has noted, the Personal Responsibility and Opportunity Act (the current form of welfare) begins with the statement:

> Marriage is the foundation of a successful society. Marriage is an essential institution of a successful society which promotes the interest of children. Promotion of fatherhood and motherhood is integral to successful childrearing and the well-being of children. (17)

A CENTURY OF "DESERVING" MOTHERS AND WELFARE: WHO GETS WHAT?

Tracing the history of welfare reform throughout the century is a momentous task and one that has been well documented by many researchers (Abramovitz 1988, 2000; Mink 1999; Cocoran et al., 2000). My goal here is then not to reinvent the wheel, but to highlight the major gendered tenets of welfare policies in order to better understand the ideological underpinnings of how working poor single mothers are "undeserving" of such supports. By drawing on previous analyses of public policy this distinction between "deserving" and "undeserving" mothers becomes paramount in the debate and demonstrates the stigmatization of working poor mothers (and poor mothers in general) within the system. As such my analysis does not offer a new historical account of welfare, but instead draws together existing work. In doing so, I set the sociohistorical framework for rethinking welfare and workforce development in the ensuing chapters in ways that attend to and address the criticisms that have been waged against such programs.

When we apply a gendered lens to welfare programs, it becomes clear that one of the original impetuses of these programs was to create a support net for single mothers at the turn of the twentieth century[8] because of a fear that if single mothers entered the workforce there would be an increased number of delinquent children and, perhaps more important, that women would take away job opportunities from men. As such, a consequence of the early welfare policy was to keep single mothers out of the paid labor force in order to protect men's jobs and children's upbringing. To do so the government provided them with the economic supports that would allow them to survive without paid work and a man's salary. Some of the drive to support single mothers was indeed predicated on the notion that women in the workplace would challenge gendered assumptions regarding appropriate jobs for men and women, or perhaps more aptly stated, that women would enter into higher-paying male dominated jobs. This argument prevailed even though the labor market was and still is highly sex segregated (Abramovitz, 2000). Indeed Alice Kessler-Harris (2001) noted that turn of the century America "shared a sense of social order that accommodated job assignments by sex as they deferred to racial and ethnic hierarchies" (25).

Women comprised 25 percent of the 1900 labor market. Amongst the group of working women, almost 40 percent were either immigrants or daughters of immigrants, and 20 percent were African American (Kessler-Harris 2001, 25). The most common jobs for immigrant women of color were in domestic services, and for white women were in factories and mills (Reskin and Padavic, 2002). These jobs were low wage, with little or no possibly for advancement, and were physically and emotionally draining. Advancement into male dominated occupations would evidently have improved the economic status of women at the turn of the century. There then needed to be a mechanism to prevent women from entering the high-paying male jobs and to keep the 5.3 million employed women in 1900 (many of whom were working poor women supporting their families), seg-regated into predominately female low-paying work (Abramovitz, 2000).

To help keep the labor market segregated public policy had to take a role in the larger discourse surrounding the "appropriateness" of women entering the paid labor force during the Industrial period. Alice Kessler-Harris (1982) in her social history of women and work documented how the "domestic code"—the nineteenth century ideology that put forth that the home must be a sanctuary—served to ground this policy. It was through adherence to the domestic code that women reached full femininity and this was used to deny women work opportunities. The middle class notion of glorifying the role of the wife and mother, Kessler-Harris (1982) notes, encouraged men to find ways to keep women out of the workforce to save their own jobs. "Skilled men often chose to defend their jobs and to ratio-nalize women's labor at home by invoking the need for domestic comfort. They thus became partners to the domestic code, partners in reducing women's wages and shutting them out of work" (69). Motherhood then was heralded as the vocation for women. As Adrienne Rich (1986, 33) has noted, "motherhood has a history [and] it has an ideology." It consists of social institutions and prescriptions for women's behaviors that are created by men and do not necessarily reflect all women's lives. She argues that the experiences of motherhood are directed to benefit male institutions and interests.

> Institutionalized motherhood demands of women maternal "instinct" rather than intelligence, selflessness rather than self-realization, relation to others rather than creation of self. Motherhood is "sacred" so long as its offspring are "legitimate"—that is, as long as the child bears the name of the father, who legally controls the mother. It is a "woman's highest and holiest mission," according to a socialist tract of 1914, and . . . [a] Southern historian of 1910 tells us that "woman is the embodiment of the home and the home is the basis of all institutions, the buttress of society." (42)

Turn of the century public policy was shaped by and reinforced gender ideology that attempted to keep white middle-class women out of the paid labor force and poor women of color in low-wage work. Throughout industrialization the domestic code became a permanent feature of this social ideology. The divide between public and private spheres of social life, which itself was highly gendered, would continue to ground policy throughout the century. However, this ideology of motherhood was based on a white middle-class perspective, as poor women and women of color routinely occupied both the public and private spheres of life. Reskin and Padavic (2002) clearly noted how the ideology of separate spheres was nothing more than a myth for these women, as they had to perform work in the public and private spheres in order to survive. Yet because this ideology was a feature of the labor market poor women and women of color experienced decreased labor market rewards for their work and faced barriers to higher paying jobs. Indeed there were "settled understandings about the prerogatives of white male breadwinners that underlined a highly refined sexual division of labor" (Kessler-Harris 2001, 25).

Coupled with this ideology was a conception that working women had failed as mothers—as they had to work in the paid sphere to support their families.[9] This was evidenced in the overriding fear that women in the workplace, and in particular single mothers in the workplace, would lead to a class of delinquent children. Abramovitz (2000) points out that many women were forced to house their children in orphanages because they could not economically support them and/or had no available childcare. The solution then was not to universalize childcare or raise women's wages (which would actually help all working women, not just single mothers), but instead to provide single mothers with economic supports so that they would not have to work in the paid labor market. Therefore Mothers' Pensions, instituted in 1900, were social programs that provided widows "payments for the services of motherhood" (Abramivitz, 2000, 62). As such, Kessler-Harris (2001, 13) has noted that these programs, while theoretically valuing family and caregiving, have the impact of actually restricting women's rights, particularly the right to economic citizenship, as mothers are denied access to benefits if they enter the paid labor force.[10] Further, by directing the entitlements only to widows the pensions carried with them a white middle-class moral imperative—women should stay in the home to properly care for and raise children to reinforce the domestic code. This had the drastic effect of not only deeming a woman's place in the unpaid domestic sphere, but also dividing single mothers into two groups, those deserving supports (widows) and those undeserving (unmarried, divorced, and deserted women).

The notions of "appropriateness" and "deservingness" were clearly racialized and classed. For example, the 1913 report of the Massachusetts Commission on the Support of Dependent Minor Children of Widowed Mothers clearly noted that widowed mothers would have to be women who conformed to a certain social mold. As the report states:

> By the Workman's Compensation Law aid is given to survivors upon certain fixed terms and without reference to the character of the recipients. The Commission believes, in regard to widows, that the best interest of the state could be more successfully served by a different disposition . . . It believes that aid should be given only where there are young children in a *good* family and then only in respect to them . . . Subsidy makes it feasible that children should stay with their worthy mothers in the most normal relation still possible when the father has been removed by death. It is intended not primarily for those with least adequate incomes under the present system of aid, but for the *fit and worthy poor*. (as quoted in Mink 2003, 27–28) (italics mine)

Indeed, even those who were considered among the more progressive social reformers of the early twentieth century advocated policies that supported the white middle-class domestic code. In 1915 Hannah Einstein[11] noted that as the:

... death of the breadwinner brings about very acute economic conditions. If the widow is determined to keep her family together unaided by others, she becomes a wage earner in a store or factory. Being in most cases untrained and having to compete with younger workers, she commands a relatively smaller wage. The double duties of caring for her home and children and the regular day's work often result in the breaking down of the health of the mother, causing her to neglect her children. Ultimately she is forced to admit her inability to support her family and is obliged to place her children in an institution. If she does this, we have the spectacle of a childless mother, an operative in a factory commanding scarcely a living wage, wasting her mother love in hopeless drudgery. (as quoted in Mink and Solinger, 2003, 33)

The solution, Einstein advocated, was the development of mother's pensions, which she referred to as a "remarkable development."

When the death of the breadwinner puts in jeopardy the usefulness of its future citizens it is the duty of the community to step in and prevent the interruption of the mother's maternal duties—the care and bringing up of her children. (35)

As such early welfare reform was based on the idea that single mothers should not work in the paid labor force because of their work demands in the unpaid domestic sphere. Yet, while sounding noble, the concept of the mother's pension never offered assistance to all mothers who may have qualified. As Mink and Solinger (2003) note, aid was determined based on "worthiness" of the applicant and her suitability for work. As such "these and other barriers to eligibility restricted program participation by never-married and divorced mothers, and by mothers whom racism designated as unworthy or better suited to wage work than motherhood" (42).

This thinking was clearly borne out in the data. In 1920, eight million women worked in the paid labor force. Of those women, 25 percent were married and 15 percent more were widowed, divorced, or separated (Kessler-Harris 2001, 37). A more complete analysis of the data incorporating race variables finds that while half of all married black women worked in the paid labor force of 1920, less than a quarter of their white counterparts were in the labor market. Looking across occupational data, it is clear that African-American women found themselves overwhelmingly employed in low-wage work, with 75 percent of them working as farm laborers, launderers, or domestics[12] (Kessler-Harris 2001, 43).

The tenor of deserving and undeserving single mothers, across social variables, was amplified in further reiterations of the Mothers' Pension throughout the twentieth century. In 1935 the passage of the Social Security Act "led millions of women to become dependent on the most stigmatized and limited forms of public aid—Aid to Dependent Children (ADC)" (Luker 1996, 52). ADC was based on the idea that the only women who deserved assistance were mothers and mothers only deserved the support if they were widowed, not if they "choose" to bear children outside of marriage, were divorced, or deserted. Further Kristen Luker (1996, 54) has noted ADC was "originally conceived of as a stopgap—a temporary measure that would support needy widows and their children until sufficient numbers of working fathers were covered by other insurance plans designed to protect their families when they died." Again this indicates that a woman's economic support should come from her husband and if he dies the state can come in to supplement those lost wages. Widows were quite deserving of supports as their husbands' death was out of their control (as opposed to divorce or having a child outside of marriage that seems to be clearly conceptualized as within the control of women). Widows, who were more likely to be white and middle class, then needed protections and their husbands needed a system to ensure the protection of their wives and families after death.

Of course not all single mothers were widowed, but they still needed economic supports. However the need to distinguish these women from the more deserving widows was critical to this policy discussion. As such the 1939 amendment to the Social Security Act was better able to accomplish this goal but with drastic gendered effects. With the passage of Survivors Insurance and Old Age Insurance in the 1939 amendment, widows were able to access these benefits, while unmarried, divorced, and deserted mothers were funneled onto ADC.[13] This then, for the most part, moved widows from ADC to Social Security, and kept non-widows on ADC. The 1939 amendment created a two-tiered unequal system of supports. Further, ADC payments were the only part of the Social Security Act that was not considered an entitlement because the individual is in need. In addition, payments on ADC were often substantially less than those on Social Security; were means tested where participants had to "prove" their lack of income and resources; were administered by the states, so there were not universal federal guidelines; and contained extensive behavior restrictions, including home visits (to make sure a man was not in the house) and periodic eligibility checks (Luker, 1996; Abramovitz, 1998).

While ADC was originally expected to phase out as Social Security programs grew, the reality was that the program greatly expanded during the middle and end of the twentieth century. Researchers have noted that this expansion is related in great part to the changing socioeconomic and demographic characteristics of single mothers. Specifically, 50 percent of all single mothers in 1947 were widowed, 33 percent were deserted by their husbands, 20 percent were divorced, and only half of 1 percent had never been married (Abramovitz, 1998). Today these numbers have been switched with the growing group of single mothers, those that had never been married (United States Bureau of Labor Statistics, 2002). As the marital status associated with single mothers changed over the century, so has the racial composition. Mothers Pensions and the early ADC programs (pre-1939) were directed toward white middle-class widows. However, as this group of women transitioned to Social Security programs as a result of the 1939 amendment, single mothers who had few resources or recourse other than ADC/AFDC replaced them. For example, African-American women, many of whom had to move from the South to the North as they were often displaced by the mechanization of farm work, found that they (and their partners) were ineligible for Social Security payments (as domestic and agricultural jobs were exempt from the Social Security Act).[14] They then only had one option left, to apply for ADC. As such African-American women and other women of color, began to comprise the bulk of ADC rolls.

By the middle of the twentieth century a two-tiered system was firmly in place in the United States. "Respectable" white middle-class widows were able to access Social Security supports and "undeserving" single mothers, often poor and of color, collected ADC. This system served to divide women on the basis of marital status, race, and class. ADC represented those women who had failed at middle-class values—they could not secure a husband who earned breadwinner wages. As Mink (1993) notes, at the core of racialized and gendered welfare politics is the stereotype of the black welfare mothers. Senator Moynihan's 1965 report *The Negro Family* traced welfare dependency to the structure of the black family "in which the black woman behaved badly—first by having illegitimate children, then by presiding over the family and thereby undermining the position of the man" (Mink, 1993, 672). The stage was set and in motion to stigmatize welfare recipients as poor, lazy, and of color.

WELFARE AND WORK

As the development of a two-tiered system of public assistance was institutionalized in the middle of the twentieth century certain ideological beliefs became codified in these policies. Recall that the original conception of Mothers Pensions was a "payment for services of motherhood" (Abramovitz 2000, 62). At some level there was an acknowledgement (however misguided in terms of the reasons for supporting it) of the importance of women's domestic labor to both the family and society. The shift to ADC began to move the focus away from the work associated with being a mother, as the recipients increasingly represented poor women and women of color. No longer were payments to support the unpaid work of mothers, now the women receiving supports under ADC had to work outside the home. In fact in the 1940s and 1950s many states forced women to work by lowering payments and restricting eligibility requirements of ADC (Abramovitz 2000, 70). Yet at the same time as poor women and women of color were being forced to work in the paid labor market, white middle-class women were being told that they should not work in the paid labor market. In fact, not only should white middle-class women not engage in paid labor, if was believed that if they did it could easily lead to the destruction of their families and communities. This was drastically illustrated in a 1955 *Ladies Home Journal* article that "warned the American woman that her children will hate her if she works" (Soligner 1999, 14).

So while poor mothers were being forced into the paid labor market, middle-class mothers were being forced out of it (or told not to enter at all). How did these two seemingly contradictory messages for women coexist? The answer is actually quite simple and is directly related to the need for cheap labor in an expanding U.S. service sector. Post–World War II, as middle-class women were told it was their "patriotic" duty to quit their job so that it would be available for a returning solider, the growing number of service jobs, including jobs in childcare, cleaning, cooking, and secretarial work, needed to be filled. Luckily for service sector industries there was a ready-made labor force. Many of these jobs would be performed predominately by women of color, working class, and poor women who were either single or whose male partners could not financially support their families. So throughout the 1950s and 1960s women collecting welfare were forced into paid work in the growing service sector, competing with poor and working-class women who were already in those jobs. The core result was the creation of service sector industries staffed by mostly working class, poor, and minority women to provide forms of service labor to mostly white middle-class women.

The racialized and classes dimensions of these policies continued to be exaggerated in regard to work policies. Fox-Piven and Cloward (1993) in their social history of welfare, cite numerous examples of "Workfirst" pro-grams in the middle part of the twentieth century that funneled poor women of color into low-wage work. For example, during hearings at the 1967 United States Commission on Civil Rights in Jackson, Mississippi, it was unearthed that "welfare recipients in Mississippi's 'work experience' program . . . were assigned to private entrepreneurs who, according to testimony, were told to 'use them any way you can.' As a result, women were given 'work experience' in dishwashing and heavy cleaning, in haul-ing gravel and cutting grass" (129). Further, in testimony before the same commission in Indiana, one recipient, in response to the department's domestic service training program, noted "it seems rather unnecessary for a Negro to go to school to get a certificate to clean up someone else's home" (129).

The interplay of race, gender, and work was quite evident in the South-ern states. Fox-Piven and Cloward (1993) demonstrated that when ADC was implemented many states enacted provisions that were designed to keep women of color (particularly black women) in the labor pool. For example, Louisiana in 1943 adopted the first "employable mother" rule requiring that if the mother was employable in the fields, the family would be denied Aid to Families with Dependent Children payments (134). Other states followed suit and made it clear that "any job was enough," a senti-ment that persists today. So Georgia, in 1952, denied assistance to mothers who were deemed employable if suitable employment was available. Not only did suitable employment translate to any job at any wage, but Georgia rules compounded the issue by prohibiting welfare departments from sup-plementing that wage if it fell below the welfare grant levels. Moreover, in order then to keep poor women and women of color in the labor force they were also given less money than their white counterparts. For example, in 1961 the median monthly payment to blacks was $24.40, while whites received $30.40 (137).[15] While these practices were most prevalent in the South, they also were practiced in the North, resulting in the forcing of poor women of color into low-wage work throughout the country.

Driven then by a need for cheap labor, a public relations campaign ensued where welfare recipients of ADC were painted as "living well off the system" and "needed to be put to work." Indeed, unlike assistance pro-grams for the elderly or blind, often work was required as part of the pack-age (Kittay, 1998; Fox-Piven and Cloward, 1993). The changes in the 1960s and 1970s associated with the development of AFDC led to the guaranteed creation and existence of a cheap labor pool of working class and poor women who would provide the work of the service sector for low wages and no benefits. In the 1970s and 1980s as white, educated women entered the professions in greater numbers the work and family conflicts they experienced called for the need for more purchased services. The service sector continued to grow with working class and poor women of color comprising a large portion of the labor pool. Coupled with this were more stringent eligibility requirements for AFDC (and eventually its replacement Temporary Aid to Needy Families), that working poor women found themselves earning too much to qualify for public assistance programs. A clearly unspoken, but apparent goal of welfare was to get poor women a job, but not just any job, as more often than not it was a low-wage job.

Indeed the funneling of poor women and women of color into work became law in the late 1990s. Mink and Solinger (2003) note that in 1996 when President Clinton signed the Personal Responsibility and Work Opportunities Reconciliation Act (PROWA) it further "codified the view that welfare policy should reward and punish the intimate decisions and behaviors of poor single mothers" (536). The "Workfirst" model of welfare removed any notion that welfare was a social entitlement and decreased any opportunity to receive education and skills training. PROWA's assistance program, TANF, set a two-year limit to find paid work and a five-year lifetime limits on an individual receiving federally funded cash benefits. Further, participants had to work for their assistance, as TANF was based on the idea that paid work was better than welfare, education, or motherhood for this group of women. In doing so it forced welfare recipients into low-wage work and kept women funneled into traditionally female low-paying service jobs without the opportunity to improve their lives. One clear example of this is the increased dependence on welfare recipients to fill childcare labor demands. As Dorothy Roberts (1999, 162) has noted childcare is a growing occupation among TANF mothers, with 80 percent of for-profit childcare centers employing welfare recipients. And, of course, childcare is also one of the lowest paying jobs, with salaries around $13,000 annually (Roberts 1999, 162) and often with no health or pension benefits. Roberts (161) suggests how a political cartoon in the *Boston Globe* summarized this contradiction. The cartoon featured a politician talking to a woman with two young children. The politician was holding a document labeled "Welfare Reform" and the conversation in the cartoon was:

Politician: "You are a bad mother."

Welfare Mother: "Why?"

Politician: "You hang around the house taking care of the kids. We'll cut you off if you don't take a job."

Welfare Mother: "Doing what?"

Politician: "Taking care of someone else's kids." (161)

The 1996 Personal Responsibility and Work Opportunities Act (PROWA), heralded in many circles as a successful program, actually had the effect of flooding many poor women and women of color into the low-wage job market. While many welfare recipients moved into paid work, the reality was that the work was often at the lowest rungs of the occupational distribution. This trend continues into the present day. On average, in 2001, wages for single mothers with less than a high school degree were $7.20 an hour (Levitan and Gluck, 2003), not enough to raise a family out of poverty. The forced time limits and the "work or lose your benefits" mentality then provided women little choice but to accept low-wage work. Frances Fox-Piven (1999) has argued that welfare is a labor market institution that systematically alters the wage terms of the lowest levels of the labor market, creating the floor of wages. As women "roll off" welfare and welfare itself becomes more stigmatized, poor women will move from "welfare recipients" to "working poor," joining the ranks of the millions of women already in that category and not surviving economically.

What welfare reform did accomplish was provide employment for former recipients at the lowest wage levels of the market. The vast majority of welfare recipients enter the labor market at $5.50 to $6.50 an hour, and increase their wages only if they increase their hours (Negrey, Um'rani, Golin, and Gault, 2000). Further, through its historical precedence of institutionalizing a gendered two-tiered system of supports, welfare policies stigmatize poor women who access these supports and conceptualize any sense of dependency on the state as socially reprehensible, making it less likely and feasible for women to access these benefits. Coupled with this are tighter means-tested eligibility requirements determined at the state level and lifetime time limits on benefits that simply make more women less eligible for public assistance. As Sharon Hays (2002) has argued "work requirements were in effect punishments directed at single mothers who were divorced or had children outside of marriage. The punishment was having to work in low-wage jobs" (18).

WORKING POOR WOMEN, EDUCATION, AND POLICY

As the previous section demonstrated, the gendered and racialized constructions of welfare have disadvantaged women, and in particular poor women and women of color, in their quest for economic self-sufficiency and have trapped them, for the most part, in low-wage jobs. Past and current policies serve to often deprive women the opportunity to receive the education and skills training they need to secure a good job at good pay. Indeed, as Sklar, Mykyta, and Wefald (2001, 161) have argued, welfare reform itself has undermined further education and skills training. This is directly tied to the strong emphasis on "WorkFirst" and finding any job, at the expense of education and training. The focus solely on jobs only has not paid off for welfare recipients. Sklar et al. (2001) note that less than 4 percent of workfare participants end up employed in regular jobs, and often those who do find work are concentrated in low-level minimum wage work. Anthony Carnevele (1999, 43) succinctly notes that "public policy promises 'college first' to the most advantaged and 'Workfirst' at hard labor for everyone else."

Yet as the previous chapter demonstrated, access to education and training helps to increase economic self-sufficiency, while federal programs that just move participants from welfare to work tend to only moderately improve income levels and do not lessen welfare dependency (Kossek, Huber-Yoder, Castellino, and Lerner, 1997). So while education and job training can help improve the wages of low-income women, "fewer women have access to meaningful job training and education because of work requirements, time limits, and the limits on the proportions of people who can participate in programs. In addition, it has become less feasible for women to balance work, training, childcare, and other responsibilities" (Negrey, Um'rani, Golin, and Gault, 2000, 350).

So the important question is then how do we incorporate lifelong education into welfare and workforce development policies that have continually problematized single working poor mothers and forced them into work. Albeda and Tilly (1997), among others, have long argued that education will only work if there is an investment in both significant training (such as postsecondary training and/or training directly tied to the labor market needs of local employers), and if that training is accompanied by supports (such as childcare and transportation). Not only will training for training's sake not improve women's lives, neither will training and education that does not acknowledge the everyday lives of working poor women. New models must be advanced that challenge the gendered, racialized, and classed nature of existing public policies by incorporating meaningful education into the lives of working women, along with comprehensive supports that are aimed at raising individuals out of poverty.

The next chapter focuses on one such policy initiative in New Jersey that attempted to address the educational needs of working poor single mothers by providing them with education and training via the Internet in their homes. What is critical to focus on is that this program is an example of workforce development policies that address the gender/racialized/classed notions of the previous policies. First, it puts the role of education upfront. Investing in human capital via education and skills training will lead to long-term self-sufficiency improvements. In doing so, it also takes into account the barriers that single working mothers face—childcare, transportation, inflexible schedules—and attempts to minimize or eradicate them. Further, and perhaps more important, it exemplifies the need to reorganize workforce development systems to better attend to the needs of all workers.

NOTES

1. For a full discussion of intersectional approaches, see Browne and Misra, 2003.

2. Berger and Luckman (1972) coined the term "the social construction of reality" in which they suggest that social reality is dialectically constructed via processes of externalization, objectification, and internalization. The result is the divorcing of actions and beliefs from the social processes that created them.

3. This is a 2001 update of Abramovitz's (1983) article, "Everyone Is on Welfare."

4. This was terminology coined during welfare reform of 1996 under President Clinton.

5. The self-sufficiency standard calculates the minimum cost of living and takes into account costs relating to basic housing, childcare, food, transportation, healthcare, and taxes. In addition, the standard also takes into account any benefits accrued via the Earned Income Tax Credit, the Childcare Tax Credit, and the Child Tax Credit (Pierce and Brooks, 2002).

6. A county where New Jersey piloted the online program. See chapter 4 for a full discussion of this project.

7. Full-time minimum wage in 2002 was $5.15 an hour. This figure includes

the net effects of the Earned Income Tax Credit and the subtraction of taxes (Pierce and Brooks, 2002).

8. Clearly gendered and racialized notions of public policy infused welfare reform pre-twentieth century. While this is beyond the scope of my work, I refer the interested reader to Fox Piven and Cloward (1993) and Mink (1999) for a comprehensive historical discussion.

9. As Reskin and Padavic (2004) note working-class men and men of color who could not support their families without their wives incomes were also viewed as having failed at attaining masculinity in society.

10. Kessler-Harris (2001) extends this argument to suggest that this paradigm continues today as welfare recipients and low-wage workers lack the services (adequate daycare, efficient public transportation, etc.) that enable full labor market participation (13).

11. Hannah Einstein (1862–1929) was a social worker instrumental in organizing the Widowed Mother Fund Association to support widowed mothers so that they may devote themselves full time to childrearing (Encyclopedia Britannica, Inc., 1999).

12. Interestingly these data highlighting racial discrimination led to social reform that focused on issues of developing job opportunities for black men, not equality for black women. Many African American organizers of the early 1900's advocated for women's domestic roles, not workplace opportunities. For example, Kessler-Harris (2001, 44) notes that "Marcus Garvey's influential black nationalist movement argued that women should give up their jobs in order to sustain the masculinity of their partners . . . the Brotherhood of Sleeping Car Porters, a highly successful labor organization, actively discouraged wives from working, its members sharing with their wives an ideology of masculine providerhood and female domesticity that closely resembled that of skilled white trade unionists, as well as middle class whites."

13. ADC was eventually replaced by Aid to Families with Dependent Children (AFDC).

14. The racial divide in regard to welfare policies cannot be understated. Albeda and Tilly (1997), among others, note that the Social Security Act perpetuated a racial double standard that continues to exist today. The act's core programs— Unemployment Compensation and Old Age Assistance—excluded agricultural workers and domestic servants. These occupations were primarily occupied by black workers in the South (91).

15. This data refers to individuals living in cities with populations of 50,000 to 500,000 persons.

4

POLICY AND PROGRAMS: SINGLE WORKING POOR MOTHERS AND ONLINE LEARNING

Public policy has a history of not attending to the experiences of women, and in particular single poor mothers of color, and instead typically divides women along race, class, and marital status lines. As a result these policies often fall short of raising women out of poverty. There then needs to be alternative programs and policies advanced that take into account the experiences of women, and are not based on gendered assumptions. This chapter presents one such program implemented in New Jersey that used online learning to deliver skills training to single working poor mothers.

The New Jersey project was unique for many reasons. First, the New Jersey program was one of only a handful of programs in which the mode of skills delivery—online learning—acknowledged that individuals need training alternatives that provide the flexibility that is not available in the traditional classroom setting. Second, this project attended to a demographic group at which public sector programs are often not directed—the working, and specifically, single working poor mothers. This was a momentous step in the state's workforce development system. The New Jersey One-Stop Career Center system, instituted under the federal Workforce Investment Act, has as its mandate to develop programs to provide individuals with high-level demand skills so that they can be placed in high-wage jobs. Implicit in this argument is that once one "rolls" off of welfare and is placed in a job, that job will be high-wage enough to allow them to support themselves and will have career ladders that will allow them to continue to advance. As noted in previous chapters, this workforce policy is predicated on the erroneous idea that once one leaves welfare or graduates high school they will be in a position to economically support themselves. The New Jersey pilot program, providing job training via online learning to single working poor mothers, challenged these assumptions. Not only did State Labor Department officials acknowledge that being placed in a job does not lead to self-sufficiency but, more important, if public sector job training is to have any positive effects on raising workers skills, job training itself needs to be reconceptualized.

In this chapter I present the experiences of the women as they began and completed their program to illustrate how public policy, while taking gender into account, can effectively address the needs of working women. The goal of this chapter is not to simply summarize the New Jersey online learning project, but instead to demonstrate how a workforce development program can be successful if it attends to the lived experiences of women. By drawing on qualitative data from the women in the program I demonstrate how work, family, and education demands can be effectively integrated in a workforce development system.

DEMOGRAPHICS OF WORKING POOR SINGLE MOTHERS AND EFFECTS ON POLICY

To begin it is helpful to understand the demographic composition of single mothers in the United States. Indeed when we focus on single mothers in comparison to married mothers several key trends emerge that help explain single mother's increased rate of poverty and the inability of current policy to address their poverty. First, single mothers are drastically affected by what Albeda and Tilly (1996) have referred to as the "triple whammy." The first vector in this whammy is that the gender wage gap penalizes a woman's pay from the start, costing her at least 25 cents for every dollar her male counterpart earns. Second, because women perform the bulk of the unpaid household labor themselves, single mothers need jobs that offer them flexibility to take care of their childcare and family needs, and will often sacrifice pay and job variety for even the smallest degree of flexibility. Finally, the single mother is the only earner in her family. Quite simply, the more earners a family have, the more the family income.

The "triple whammy" clearly disadvantages single mothers. In addition, Levitan and Gluck (2003) have documented that single mothers are disadvantaged when it comes to possessing the characteristics typically associated with success in the labor market. In the United States, married mothers are twice as likely as single mothers to have a four year college degree (11). In addition, 50 percent of single mothers are women of color, as compared to only about 28 percent of married mothers. Further, single mothers tend to be younger than married mothers, indicating that they have less years in the paid workforce (11–13). Perhaps even more significant is that single mothers tend to be employed in low-wage industries and occupations. Just under half of single mothers work in service industries and almost 20 percent of single mothers work in retail trade industries (29–30). Within the service sector the major employers include healthcare, educational, business, and social services. In fact service occupations account for nearly 25 percent of single mothers employment (as opposed to only 15 percent of married mothers jobs). Coupling the industry distribution with an occupational distribution confirms that single mothers are overrepresented in low-wage jobs. In the service sector single mothers often labor as janitors, cafeteria workers, security guards, home health care aides, private household workers, orderlies, and childcare workers (Levitan and Gluck, 2003). These jobs are low paying and often do not offer employer-sponsored pensions or health insurance. In addition to service occupations single mothers are also highly represented in administrative occupations, as 23 percent of single mothers are employed in these jobs. In contrast only 13 percent of single mothers are employed in managerial and executive occupations and 16 percent are employed in professional and technical occupations (29–30).

With this demographic picture in place it is clear that current policy needs to be more innovative and inclusive in its approach to raise women out of poverty. Under PROWA job training and education are treated as "short term job readiness training and immediate work placement, instead of longer educational investments" (Negrey, Um'rani, Golin, and Gault, 2000, 350). In addition, coupled with increased work requirements, limits on the proportions of individuals that can participate in job training, and a lack of childcare, few women can find the time to further their education. Again this only applies to the working poor who have qualified for welfare. Women without the safety net of welfare have an even more difficult time attempting to further their education.

BARRIERS TO SKILLS TRAINING

Based on this demographic composite a significant challenge is increasing the *access* to skills training for low-wage working mothers. Indeed the workforce system faces significant obstacles in regard to how to deliver skills training to this group. This population faces many barriers that prevent them from attaining skills training via traditional modes of delivery.[1] Foremost, childcare needs place a burden on single mothers that often precludes them from attending traditional education programs (Edin and Lein, 1997; Johnson, 2002). Locating affordable childcare and "off hours" childcare (such as on nights and weekends when many classes are offered) often proves to be a daunting task. In addition, a large percentage of single working mothers are employed in jobs with irregular schedules, such as those characteristic of the service sector, making it difficult to attend classes that are inflexible in their scheduling. This is further complicated because most organizations that provide training typically are not open after traditional work hours or on weekends (Miller, Molina, Grossman, and Golanka, 2004).

In addition to childcare needs and irregular schedules, transportation also proves to be a significant barrier for many single mothers, making it difficult for them to attend classes. Nationally, one-third of households earning less than $15,000 a year do not own a car (Van Horn and Schaffner, 2003). This is especially relevant in suburban and rural areas where there are not extensive public transportation systems. Furthermore, noncollege educated workers often find very little access to employer-sponsored training. Lisa Lynch and Sandra Black (1995) found that employers' investment decisions in regard to employee training are influenced by the characteristics of the workers that they employ. Overall, they found that employees who are perceived as having a high turnover rate and/or possess lower levels of formal education are less likely to receive employer provided training. As such workers either forego training opportunities, or spend years attempting to complete credentials or degrees by taking one to two classes every few months. As a result of the many obstacles facing single mothers it is evident that alternatives to the traditional delivery method of skills training must be explored and institutionalized in order to increase the skill levels of this population.

OVERVIEW OF THE NEW JERSEY ONLINE LEARNING PROGRAM

The New Jersey State Department of Labor and Workforce Development developed and implemented an online learning program for 128 underemployed single women with at least one child under seventeen years old, earning 250 percent or less of the poverty line, and living in one of five Workforce Investment Board (WIB) areas covering eight counties. This program provides participants with a computer (desktop or laptop), printer, Internet access, and skills training courses[2] for a year. Upon successful completion of the program, the participants were able to keep their computers.

While each of the WIB developed their own programs there were some basic similarities in each area. Each WIB had an on-site orientation (held at the One-Stop Career Center or a local community college) that introduced the women to the program and provided them with their equipment. Each woman was assigned a job coach in order to ensure that the skills she was acquiring were directly tied to her career and educational goals and the local job market. In addition, each woman had access to twenty-four hour technical and education support (typically provided through the educational provider) and in-person support at the One-Stop Career Center. As such, each woman was integrated into the services of the One-Stop Career Center, and was able to access the employment services available there.

WHO ARE THE WOMEN IN THE NEW JERSEY PROGRAM?

The 128 women in the New Jersey pilot program represent a diverse population of working poor single mothers. For many of them this was the first time they accessed any public sector supports. They arrived at this program from a variety of sources—flyers strategically placed throughout town, newspaper articles and advertisements, word of mouth from friends and employers, and referrals from individuals associated with the local employment and training system. As is evident from the following demographic composite they represent a growing slice of the American pie that is working, but "getting by on the minimum" (Johnson, 2001).

Table 1 details some of the main demographic characteristics of the participants. The average age of the women is 32 years old; with the youngest women aged 20 years old, and the oldest women aged 54. These low-wage workers are thus not teenagers working for "spending" money, but adults working for life's necessities. The women also represent diversity in regard to race/ethnicity, which closely mirrors the distribution of the working poor.

Table 4.1   Demographic Breakdown of Participants

County	County 1	County 2	County 3	County 4	County 5	All Counties
Participants	21	23	17	39	28	**128**
Age						
Low Age	20	22	22	21	48	**20**
High Age	54	49	46	50	20	**54**
Average Age	36	33	34	29	26	**32**
Ethnicity						
African American	12	7	9	24	18	**56**
Hispanic	4	9	3	4	6	**24**
White	5	7	5	10	4	**47**
Asian	0	0	0	0	0	**0**
Native American	0	0	0	1	0	**1**
Highest Education Attained						
Less than a High School Degree	1	0	0	6	0	**7**
High School Degree/GED	13	15	8	14	18	**68**
Associate Degree			1	10	7	**18**
Some college	5	6	2	7	4	**24**
Bachelor Degree	0	0	3	0	3	**6**
Technical Certification* some women reported in both HS and technical categories	1	2	2	6	4	**15**
Graduate Degree	1	0	1	0	0	**2**
Marital Status						
Single	15	13	10	32	14	**84**
Divorced	3	5	5	5	7	**25**
Separated	3	5	2	2	7	**19**
Personal Characteristics						
Disabled (either physical or learning)	1	2	1	1	2	**7**
English as a Second Language	4	0	4	2	9	**19**
Average Number of Children	2	2	2	2	2	**2**
Primarily Use Public Transportation	5	1	1	15	5	**27**
Own a Car or Use a Family Member's Car	16	22	16	24	23	**101**
Income Information (Yearly)						
Highest Income	30,000	26,000	40,000	43,000	30,000	**43,000**
Lowest Income	14,000	11,000	9,000	5,700	12,000	**5,700**
Mean Income	20,700	18,600	23,500	19,400	18,000	**16,900**

Table 4.1   (Continued)

County	County 1	County 2	County 3	County 4	County 5	All Counties
Median Income	21,000	20,400	21,500	13,850	15,000	**18,500**
Past Internet/Distance Learning (DL)						
Taken DL Courses Before Program	5	0	0	0	1	**6**
Used Internet Before the Program	21	18	14	35	12	**100**
Used E-mail Before the Program	19	19	7	28	17	**90**
Used Chat Rooms Before the Program	5	7	10	22	17	**61**
FTP Files Before the Program	10	3	3	13	11	**40**

Fifty-six women are black, 24 are Hispanic, 47 are white, and one is Native American. In regard to educational attainment, the majority of women (68 of them) are high school graduates or earned a GED. Further 18 women hold associates degrees; 24 women attended college; 6 women have a college degree; 15 women have some type of technical certification; and 2 women have graduate degrees from universities outside of the United States.[3] In fact only seven women did not graduate high school. This continues to demonstrate that the working poor, for the most part not only possess education, but as I will illustrate later in this chapter, value education in their lives.

While all women in the pilot program have incomes of 250 percent or less of the poverty line,[4] the average annual income of the women is $16,900; with the highest income in our sample of $43,000, and the lowest income of $5,700. The income data clearly show that the women are for the most part working in minimum wage (or close to minimum wage) jobs. This is the point that cannot be understated. It does not matter that they are earning an income because it is not enough of an income for them to support themselves and their children. Once one takes into account the costs associated with their employment—childcare, transportation, healthcare—along with the daily costs of living (food, housing, etc), they are as poor as the unemployed.

The income data is clearly related to the women's occupational distribution. As demonstrated in Table 1 the women are employed in a variety of industries and occupations, most of which characterize the low-wage labor market. Many women (58 of them) work in administrative office positions such as secretaries, receptionists, and office assistants. Women in the sample are also employed in the growing service sector. Twenty-seven of the women work in retail sales/restaurants/housecleaning; and fifteen women work in childcare and daycare. Sixteen women in the program work in the health care industry in such jobs as Certified Nursing Assistants, dietary aides, and medical assistants. There are also three women who work in factories, two women who are employed as bus drivers, five women who are bank tellers, and one mail carrier.

Interestingly, the women in the program also represent diversity in regard to variables associated with learning techniques relative to online learning. Seven women in the pilot program have disabilities; for nineteen women, English is their second language; and twenty-seven women do not own a car and use public transportation. Further, the women in the sample entered the program with a range of experience with computers and the Internet. One hundred women accessed the Internet prior to this program most accessing through library programs and workplaces, ninety women have used e-mail, sixty-one women have entered chat rooms, but only forty women have sent a file though e-mail (FTP). These data indicate that while many women are familiar with the basics of computers and the Internet, less than one-third of the women have used the computer for more advanced purposes, such as file transfers. In addition, for close to 20 percent of the women in the pilot program, this was the first time they accessed the Internet and other forms of information technology.

BARRIERS TO TRADITIONAL EDUCATION VENUES

As is evident from the data capturing the participants' previous computer usage, online learning was uncharted territory for almost all the participants. Only 6 of the 128 women had taken distance learning courses previously, and these courses were predominately via the postal mail or television, and not the computer. Yet this does not indicate that the women were uninterested in continuing their education. Instead, as I found, they often faced sets of barriers that made it difficult to complete educational programs.

Indeed, much of our public media bemoans the lack of value that the working poor place on education (Newman, 1999). However as many researchers on poverty have noted this commonplace conception is flawed. For example, Katherine Newman (1999) in her study of low-wage workers in Harlem found that not only did the workers value education, they also saw it as an avenue out of low-wage work. The same can be said of the women I studied in New Jersey. The women in the pilot project are, for the most part, planning to return to school to work toward a formalized degree, be it a GED, associate, or bachelor. However, many of the women see numerous obstacles, most commonly childcare demands, which prevent them from achieving that goal in the near future. For instance, a woman told me that, "I was trying to go to school but it was too hard because of my daughter and having someone to watch her." Many other women reiterated this challenge in regard to educational attainment. For example one woman stated that, "I want to go to college but I don't see it being something that would fit in my life now because of the kids, money, and not much time."

The challenges associated with childcare are further reinforced when one examines the household composition of the women in the pilot program. A significant majority of the women, sixty-nine of them, lived alone with their children. They truly were the only full-time care provider in the home. Fifteen women lived with their children and an adult family member (overwhelmingly among this group it was the women's own mother), while six women lived with their partners and their children. Of course, simply having another adult in the home does not mean that the domestic responsibility was equally shared.[5] Finally for six of the women in the training program, not only did they provide care for their own children, they were also the primary caregivers for non-biological children (one woman provided care for her children's children, and five women provided care for other relative's children). As such, the need to care for others (and particularly one's own children) clearly serves as a major barrier to attaining training and education, indicating how the gendered nature of caring labor serves as a barrier to a woman's ability to reach self-sufficiency.

In addition to balancing school and family demands, women saw other obstacles to their education success, such as financial constraints. One woman reported that, "I would like to do my master's degree but I don't have the money, so I cannot afford it."

Women further reported that they were apprehensive about returning to school. A participant told me that, "I would like to take college courses but I'm afraid. I'm hoping to gain confidence through this program."

Interestingly, all the obstacles that prevent the women from furthering their education are minimized and sometimes even eliminated by a public sector job training program using online learning. Further, regardless of the reason or reasons that women in the pilot program have postponed furthering their education, they all see the online learning program as an initial step in their educational attainment. This was a significant point for working poor single mothers in the New Jersey project. They saw the value of continued education and skills training, but could not achieve it along the traditional timetable. This points to the necessity of not only alternative educational routes that are meaningful, efficient, and accepted by employers, but an upfront acknowledgement of the demands of women's lives in policy formation.

REASONS FOR ENROLLING IN AN ONLINE LEARNING PROGRAM

While each woman enrolled in the pilot program for a variety of individual reasons, there are some common threads among their explanations. Clearly the relationship between high level skills and higher wages was paramount as many women reported that they joined the program in order to gain a skill set that would allow them to qualify for a job that provides self-sufficiency wages. For example, one participant told me that this program could help her advance in her current job. "I am only a clerk typist and I need to make more money, and my boss was pleased with me and suggested this program." Another woman reported that she enrolled in this program in order to change jobs within her workplace. "I wanted to participate in this program to enhance my computer skills so that I can get certification in computers and I can make a lateral move in my job."

In addition to advancing within their jobs, many women reported that this program would provide them with the skills necessary to change jobs in order to increase their earnings. For example, a woman felt she was stuck in her current job and told me:

My mom saw an ad in the newspaper about this program, and because I have been with my company so long and there is no room for advancement because I work at a car dealership, I thought that through this program, I could learn computer programs and get more training and look for a better job.

While several women mirroring her sentiment reported that they were located in jobs without opportunities for advancement, other women noted that they entered the program because they were ready to change jobs. One woman reported that "I went through the workforce and I have been doing nursing for twenty years and I am looking for something different."

Women also enrolled in the program for the opportunities to receive training and certifications in Microsoft Office products.[6] They believed the certification would be a credential that they could use to either increase their pay in their current job or find a higher paying job. A participant felt that this program is "an opportunity for me to advance and obtain a certificate. I am self-taught on the computer but need certification." The ability to get official Microsoft certifications and training were clearly a driving force behind many of the women's reasons for entering the program. A woman summed it up for us when she reported that, "I've been trying to get computer training and this was a great opportunity."

As evident from the women, they were well aware of their status in the workplace and knew, at least in general, what they would need to improve that status. Be it attaining further education, credentials, or changing jobs they knew that something had to change in their lives in order for them to improve their economic situation. Yet while they had the general information they did not have the specific details about how to accomplish this. It is then critical for public sector training programs to provide specific data and interventions not just on labor market trends, but also on creating educational programs and career paths that will lead to self-sufficiency.

In addition to providing workplace skills and credentials this program also offered women the chance to obtain general computer skills and Internet access. One participant told us that she believed the program would provide her with both the opportunity and equipment to learn more about the Internet in her home.

> The program seemed interesting and I wanted to have Internet access to better my career. I've been going to the library to teach myself computers already so these courses will help me. I have a young son and he is already on the computer at school.

Other women reported that this program would provide them with an opportunity to access to computers that they did not have elsewhere. One woman stated, "I want to be a success and know that I need to learn the computer. My child knows the computer better than me. I feel like I am missing part of life."

This is a point that cannot be understated. When the women enrolled in the program words such as "World Wide Web," "blogs," "dot.com," and "instant messaging" were part of the lexicon of the computer literate, and had infiltrated the everyday vernacular of much of the media. While 80 percent of the participants in this program had some experiences with the Internet, these interactions were quite limited in scope. The women believed that they were being left behind of a great technological revolution. Perhaps even more disconcerting to them was not only were they being left behind in the computer age, but so were their children.

As such women also reported that they enrolled in this program in order to help increase their family literacy. A woman told us, "I use computers at work and don't own a computer. My daughter loves computers and we don't have one." Another woman reiterated this point.

> I think it could benefit me and my children. It gives me an opportunity to learn more computer skills and gives my daughter access and opportunities that she wouldn't have before.

In addition, the women reported that by completing their job training at home they can also serve as role models for their children. A woman told us that:

> The sole purpose of this program is being able to better myself. Anything I can get I always try to take advantage of. I have a nine-year-old girl who looks to me for everything. I need to further myself so she knows that there is a lot out there.

The need to ensure that their children know the importance of and receive educational opportunities contributed to the reasons as to why many of the women enrolled in the program. Indeed, many women felt that it was precisely when they had children that they began to see that education was an important aspect of their lives. They wanted education and skills training so that they could better their lives, but they also believed that by completing training in their homes they could demonstrate to their children that the importance of education for their futures. Indeed, many women voiced that they wanted their children to stay in school and complete their education so that they would not be stuck in a low-wage job in their adult years. Of course implicit, and sometimes explicit in the women's reasoning, was to ensure that their children did not end up like their mothers—that is, working and in poverty.

Related to this was that some of the women reported that participating in an educational program would help them gain confidence to help them further their education and advance their jobs. One told me, "I need a leg up to give me that extra edge to succeed. It is hard enough to be a woman this will give me more confidence."Another woman reiterated her point. "I am intimidated by computers, and I feel it will help me in the workforce to get a better job."

Finally women reported that they enrolled in the program because it provided them flexibility to complete their education in a way that would not conflict with their work and family demands. A woman informed me that:

I've been investigating court reporting, but I cannot attend the courses because of my daughter. Who will watch her at night? So I saw the newspaper article and thought this could be the way to go.

Another also told me that:

I'm in college but the problem is when I can take the classes because I need a sitter. I work full time and have to go [through college] slow. So I was really interested in this program.

POTENTIAL OBSTACLES

While the women I interviewed were excited about the program they were also aware that they would have to overcome some obstacles in order to succeed in an online learning environment. The most commonly reported obstacles were potential conflicts with childcare. One woman, who similar to many of the women in the program planned on doing their coursework at night while their children were sleeping, told us that her greatest obstacle was simply, "My child not sleeping through the night."

Many of the women felt that just everyday childcare would be a major obstacle to their success. Women reported that they planned to enlist the help of family and friends in providing childcare; work on their online learning courses at times when their children are not at home or when they are sleeping; or some of the women, who were provided with laptop computers, hoped to work on their courses outside the home (such as in their workplace). This raises the important point that online learning in the home is not a substitution for childcare. Instead it is a tool that can help women better manage childcare needs in relation to their education.

In addition to childcare, finding the time in their busy days to take their online courses was the next common obstacle women believed that they would have to address. For example, one participant reported that her greatest barrier to success was, "time management, when I have a hard day at work, come home, and being very tired." Another woman reiterated this concern of finding time to complete the work. "I am worried about being able to work, go to school, and do this also."

The women reported that they have begun to think of ways to overcome these potential barriers. One woman planned on scheduling time in her day when she would complete her courses. Other women wanted to make online learning part of their routine, so that it becomes one of their daily responsibilities.

Women were also concerned about potential medical problems or health concerns for themselves and their families that may impede their progress. For example, during the course of the program one woman's daughter was scheduled for surgery and as a result, much of the participant's time would be spent caring for her child. Similarly another woman reported that her daughter, who suffers from an illness, might also need extra care, taking her away from her online courses. In addition to their children's illness, some of the women report that their own health problems may contribute to slowed progress in the program.

The women also anticipated obstacles relative to the program itself. Most commonly, the women believe that technical problems may be a barrier to their success. Women were concerned that they would not be able to access help for technical and Internet problems. They were concerned about not knowing how to communicate the technical problems they would encounter effectively, or be able to successfully troubleshoot on their own.

In addition to technical help, some of the participants felt that their typing skills may be an obstacle to their success. A woman felt that "a barrier would be my typing skills. I do not type very fast, and I will need to practice and improve my typing skills."

Finally some women reported that they felt working on their online learning home alone may be a potential barrier. A woman reported that she was concerned because "there is not a support system. I will not have someone to discuss problems with the course." Related to this another woman felt that, "not having a teacher to ask questions or give directions, and being on your own is an obstacle."

Despite the many potential barriers that the women would have to confront, they were all very excited about the prospects of the program. Indeed, at the orientation sessions in which they received their computers to take home with them they were elated and eager to start their coursework. One woman reported to us how thrilled she was to be part of the program and that, "I never thought that such a program would exist for someone like me. At first I did not think it was even real!"

CAREER GOALS

As the main goal of the online learning program is to prepare women for jobs that offer advancement and high wages, it is important to assess the career goals that the women held for themselves. I found that while there is much diversity in our sample relative to career goals, several trends did emerge when I asked the women what they saw as the career opportunities available to them as a result of the skills training they would receive in this program. Women seemed to fall into three main categories of career goals that will help policymakers design programs. First, a small number of women had a definite job goal. Some of the women reported that they hoped to receive job advancements within their current organization. For example, one woman would like to be promoted to the Microsoft Technical Teacher at her office and another woman told us that was hoping to get promoted to a legal assistant in the law firm that she was employed. In these cases and similar ones, the participants reported that their current employers were supportive of the program with some of them allowing the women to work on their courses during their employment hours. This clearly could only be accomplished with an online learning program, as the women are able to sign onto the courses via the Internet from virtually anywhere. In addition to promotions within their current organization, some of the women reported that they had specific occupational goals, such as nursing, computer programmer, or computer technical help.

However, the vast majority of women did not have specific job goals, but rather had a more general picture of their future career assessment. Many of the women, while not sure of the job choice, held strong ideas on the industry that they would like to work. For instance, many of the women reported that they would like to work in the computer field, the medical field, or social service fields. Finally, some of the women were not sure what type of job or industry they saw for their future and hoped that the training they were receiving would open up opportunities for them.

The diversity of these findings point to the importance of ensuring that online training provides the women with not only hard skill attainment but also soft skills and "soft Internet skills." The women also need job coaching throughout the entirety of their training, not just at the completion. To accomplish this, part of any training program must be information about demand jobs, access to job ads via the Internet, soft skills, and job readiness.

THE SUCCESS OF ONLINE LEARNING FOR SINGLE WORKING POOR MOTHERS

The New Jersey online learning pilot project demonstrated that online learning is an effective mode of skills delivery. The participants in the project completed courses, received credentials and other formalized certificates of completion, passed Microsoft Office User Specialist (MOUS) certification, have received some job promotions and wage increases, and have an increase in self-confidence and self-esteem. In addition, there was a very high retention rate in the program, and the participants, on average, experienced wage increases. Additionally, several participants enrolled in other educational programs (such as community college and college program). Perhaps most significant, is that overwhelmingly the participants report that they would not have been able to take the classes if they were not offered online. However, several trends have emerged indicating that it is essential to attend to gender when implementing online learning for this population. That is, the experiences of the women in the pilot program highlight that online learning cannot simply be transplanted from the college model, but instead must be fashioned to take into account the structural barriers and life experiences that single working poor mothers confront.

FLEXIBILITY IN TIME AND SPACE

The vast majority of the women report that the greatest advantage of the pilot program is the flexibility that online learning offers them. They are able to work on their courses around their and their children's schedules. Emphatically, all women report that they could not complete these courses if they were not online. Yet, women find that flexibility is a double-edged sword and, in fact, there needs to be some structure in the program to ensure that they remain on target. The women suggested that they could accomplish this structure in the form of support groups (face to face), online reporting and interactions, checking into the One-Stop Career Center weekly, and completing a minimum number of hours a week.

While women need flexibility in time to complete their courses, they also need flexibility in space. Laptop computers are most effective in allowing women to have some flexibility in space. Many of the women do not have desk or office space in the home to store a desktop (especially since the computers need to be placed near electrical outlets and phone jacks), and the laptop allows them to complete their work, and then put the laptop away. In addition, with a laptop the participants can complete their coursework virtually wherever they are located and have an Internet connection. Coupling this with allowing the women to download courses to their hard drive (or, if possible, use a wireless connection),[7] would allow women to work on courses regardless of having an Internet connection at the time.

ISOLATION

Several of the women report that isolation from other students is a significant drawback of the program. One woman reported that she disliked, "not being able to have someone who understands the program right there next to you." Another woman also reported that she, "missed being able to have one on one or group discussions." Similarly a woman found that she disliked that there was, "no one to talk to right after you work on a session or someone who you can relate to about what you are going through."

In addition to being isolated from other students, women also reported that isolation from teachers and instructors was also a drawback of the program. As one woman stated, "it's hard to get help right away, and it is frustrating."

One way that two of the counties in which the New Jersey program was piloted attempted to address the issue of isolation was to provide monthly in-person support groups for the participants. Women in both of these areas felt that these groups were essential to their success in the program. One woman reported that the support groups gave her a "feeling that there is someone looking out for you." The women felt that they were not alone in cyberspace, but instead part of a community of learners. A woman reported, "when I first got started I felt dumb, but the support group develops confidence." In addition to helping increase women's confidence, the support groups also provided motivation for the women, by facilitating a healthy competition between the women in the program. The women would learn who among them was completing the most courses and try to "beat" her. A woman told me, "It helps to have competition, to see how others are going, feeling like 'hey I have to catch up.'" Furthermore, the women would also use the support groups to help each other stay with the program by providing assistance and helpful information on the program, sharing ideas and solutions to any problems they encountered, and providing verbal encouragement to each other.

The women felt that the support groups were most effective when they were structured as a blend of social activities and information sessions. They suggested that at support groups staff should share information about job skills (such as resume writing and job searching), along with strategies for succeeding in the online program (such as time management). They also felt it would be helpful to have technical and curriculum support individuals at the group meetings so that they could direct questions to them. Some women also felt it would be helpful to have pop quizzes at the support group sessions, so that they could be sure they understood what they were learning. In addition, some of the women reported that they enjoyed the support groups because they had a "theme" associated with them, such as the Thanksgiving recipe exchange. At this support group the women used their newly learned word processing skills to distribute their favorite holiday recipe to fellow participants. This more social activity was able to not only increase the women's confidence in their mastery of course content but also by sharing their work with other participants helped them feel part of a group.

The support groups in which childcare was provided offered the women the opportunities to meet with each other regularly and created a community that helped buffer some of the isolation the women reported they felt at times. The women were clear that while online chat rooms and bulletin boards[8] help to connect participants, the support groups were most effective because they were in person and not online. This finding is similar to much research on online learning that suggests that a blended model of learning (part online and part face-to-face) helps to increase student satisfaction and retention. In implementing a more blended model for the working poor population we learned that it is important to organize support groups as a flexible option, so that rigid attendance does not become an obstacle for the participants. The support groups must be arranged around the participant's schedules, which often are outside of traditional business hours, and must have childcare available for the women. In one county the support groups were held on Sunday mornings, and in another county the groups were held on weeknights.

The need for support groups was clearly voiced by the women who did not have them as part of their program. These women felt that a face-to-face monthly meeting would be very helpful for them, especially at the beginning of the program. They suggested that within the monthly meeting there should be a directed workshop (especially on job related skills). They also would like online chats or bulletin boards, and reports on the other women in the program (such as their progress and contact information), so that they would not feel as alone. They believed that this would keep them motivated and help them share information. Interestingly, some of the women who lived near each other organized impromptu support groups in their homes to help alleviate some of the isolation.

CHILDCARE AND FAMILY LITERACY

As noted earlier, while online learning helps alleviate some of the pressures of combining childcare demands and education, it is not a substitution for childcare. Women still "squeeze in" their coursework when their children are sleeping, in school, or out of the house. Clearly, having the computer in the home makes it easier for women to find time for their education and training, but it does not entirely solve childcare needs. Further, the childcare effects on online learning differ depending on the age of children. The participants report that the greatest challenges in integrating home and education demands are for older children rather than infant children. Whereas mothers of infants and young toddlers typically report that they take their online classes when their children are asleep, mothers of older children tend to find time only when their children are out of the house and do not need their intense supervision. Some of the mothers of older children spent a great deal of time attending to the extracurricular activities of their children, thereby decreasing the available time to take courses. Further, mothers of older children also had to set up boundaries with their children on sharing computer usage.[9]

There have been many positive consequences of the parent's online learning on their children as they become a role model to their children, demonstrating the importance of education in order to better their lives. A woman reported, "My children are excited about the courses, and are glad that I am going back to school."

Some of the participants have set up "family study time." One woman told us that she and her daughter share study space. They have an "L" shaped desk, the mom sits at one end and the daughter sits at the other end, and simultaneously complete their schoolwork. Further, some of the participants brought their older children into the learning process by turning to their children to help them troubleshoot the computer and help them when they had content questions. In doing so it piques the interest of the child, as one woman reported, "My son watches and reads with me . . . He wants to know what it is and why I am doing it."

In addition to role modeling and increased emphasis on education, this program brings a computer and the Internet into the homes of children who otherwise may not have access. In doing so, not only does the family's technological literacy increase, the children have opportunities that previously were unavailable. A woman reported that her teenage son, who recently dropped out of high school, used the computer to obtain his GED by completing preparatory classes online. Other women reported that their younger children used the computer to complete their homework, gain facility with the Internet, and access e-mail.

SELF-CONFIDENCE

A significant intangible result of this program is that the participants report that their self-confidence increased as a result of taking online courses. The women spoke about the program at job interviews and wanted to take more classes. A woman stated, "It has given me the confidence to be able to apply for a job knowing I have the skills they require." Another reported, "If I could pass through this program, I can continue to learn and not limit myself."

Learning how to troubleshoot the computer appeared to be one area where women experience many self-confidence gains. A woman found that, "When you understand how it works and you get familiar with it, it is wonderful!"

In addition, other people are recognizing the increased skills the women have learned in the program. A woman told me, "My confidence increased at work because I know what I am doing. It's a good feeling when people ask you and you hear them telling people, 'you're the expert.'" Another woman shared similar sentiments, "I feel more confident at work, especially when they request my help, and I'm able to help them." However, self-confidence is not only experienced at work. A woman believed that:

> I can say back in January I didn't have much knowledge in computers as I have now, which makes me feel comfortable doing my work, and that extends to my personal life.

TECHNICAL PROBLEMS

Certainly it was anticipated that technical problems would be a barrier that all participants would face. While participants in all of the online learning programs experienced technical difficulties, there are some ways that one can address the problems in a gender friendly manner. Most significantly, centralizing technical support at a local entity such as the One-Stop Career Center, and having an Information Technology expert onsite, appears to help minimize problems associated with seeking out and providing technical help. This helped to decrease the participants' discomfort with accessing technical help, personalizes the experience for the women, and decreases the time between accessing and receiving help. This method was most effective when used in conjunction with laptop computers. The participants were able to bring their laptop into the One-Stop Career Center if the problem they were experiencing could not be fixed via the phone or e-mail.

In addition to accessing technical support, the speed of the Internet connection also proved very important to effectively complete coursework. The majority of the participants are accessing the Internet via a dial-up connection. This type of connection, which is often slow, may not load Web pages correctly (especially those with many graphics) and easily disconnects. In addition to increased speed, wireless connections allow women to connect to their courses at anytime and virtually any place. Further, using wireless connections avoids the interruption of Internet service that can arise when participants home phones or cable systems are disconnected. Currently wireless connection prices are very high and not realistic within existing state budgets. However some women did receive DSL and cable modems, which were preferable to dial-up connection. Another way of addressing issues associated with being disconnected from the Internet while completing coursework, and the slow Internet connections, is the possibility of having participants download courses onto their hard drives, complete the courses off-line, and then upload the courses to the Internet.

Finally, most of the women report that there is a knowledge gap between themselves and the technical support persons. In addition to online and/or off-line workshops that could introduce women to the possible technical problems and language, it is helpful to have women work more directly with staff on technical issues, with the case manager helping to run interference with technical help desks, especially at the beginning of the program. This issue is very significant as women report that they feel intimidated to call technical help, and may decide not to reach out for help, thereby slowing down their progress.

PROJECT RETENTION AND LABOR MARKET REWARDS

For the most part the participants stayed with the program throughout its duration. There was a 92 percent retention rate in the program. Only eleven women left the program since its inception, and many of these left because of reasons unrelated to online learning. One woman left the program because she moved out of the state. A second woman was involved with a human services incident with her children, and as a result needed to focus on her children and no longer had the time for the program. She did report in an exit interview that she enjoyed the online learning experience and hoped to return to that type of learning environment. Another woman reported that a combination of childcare and work issues were the reason she left the program. This participant has a high school aged child who she needed to take to a variety of after school activities, leaving her very little time for the program. Further, she reported that her full-time job is data entry, and she did not have the energy to work on the computer when she was at home. Language barriers also caused one of the participants to drop out of the program. English is her second language, and the amount of reading needed for online learning proved to be too difficult for her.[10] Additionally, two women dropped out of the program because of learning issues relative to the online learning program. One woman felt the curriculum available through her service provider was too basic for her needs. A second woman dropped out because she did not enjoy attending the in-person support groups, and would have preferred solely online learning.

In addition the participants in the program experienced an average annual wage increase of 14 percent, and several of the participants (fifteen of them) enrolled in other educational programs (such as community college and college programs). This finding is critical, as typical cost of living increases in many jobs tend to hover around 3 to 4 percent annually. As such, women in this pilot program experienced wage increases that were an improvement over what similarly placed workers would have received.

NEXT STEPS

In many ways the New Jersey Department of Labor and Workforce Development accomplished a major coup with their online learning program for single working poor mothers. It issued computers to working poor mothers and provided education and skills training via those computers. This program was quite different than the many welfare and workforce development programs currently in existence. Not only did New Jersey direct its services to a "forgotten" group in poverty, it did so in a way that was less punitive that other public sector training programs. It entrusted the participants to get their training in their homes where they could be in control of when they completed their education. It brought the Internet and the countless sources of information that is available via the Web into the homes of individuals who typically do not have access. Further, it helps to better democratize education and training opportunities for the entire family.

Indeed the success of the participants in the New Jersey Department of Labor and Workforce Development pilot program of online learning can be attributed to several factors. These include the flexibility that online learning offered the participants in completing their coursework on their own schedule; the ways the program minimized or eliminated conflicts with childcare, transportation, and access to training itself; and the increased levels of confidence that the women reported as they achieved their goals. However, also critical to this success was that workforce development for low-wage workers was a state priority. This opened up opportunities to not only direct training to this population, but to do so in ways that attended to their life experiences. This speaks to the larger context of state government agencies' roles in addressing the needs of the workforce. As such the next chapter of this book will investigate how flexible forms of education not only must be an alternative within the workforce investment system but also be used to reformulate workforce development so that it better takes into account the needs of working women and all low-wage workers.

NOTES

1. Feminist geographers have suggested that women experience spatical entrapment that negatively affects their employment opportunities (Hanson and Johnston, 1985; Hanson and Pratt, 1995). That is, women's daily activities are spatically limited as a result of the patriarchical power relations, most notably the separation of the public and private spheres (Gilbert, 1998, 596). As such then women are less likely to be able to be able to travel to employment opportunities because of limited access to transportation and greater domestic responsibilities, and instead make employment decisions based on such factors as closeness to childcare (597). While feminist geographers have focused on employment choices, such a theoretical paradigm may also be applicable to educational opportunities.

2. The skills training centered on information technology skills and also included basic skills and life skills courses.

3. The two women who possessed graduate education both held law degrees from other countries. When they came to the United States they found themselves divorced and unable to practice law.

4. This was a requirement set by the New Jersey Department of Labor and Workforce Development.

5. See Hochschild (2003) for a discussion of the distribution of domestic labor in the home.

6. The core training that the participants received in information technology skills were Microsoft brand.

7. The New Jersey Department of Labor and Workforce Development did look into the possibility of wireless connections, but it proved to be cost-prohibitive.

8. Interestingly, although some women reported that they would like online chats and bulletin boards in the counties that did provide them they were not heavily utilized by the participants.

9. The New Jersey Department of Labor and Workforce Development did include children's software on the computers to encourage the participation of the family.

10. A potential solution to this is to provide an audio component.

5

RETHINKING WORKFORCE DEVELOPMENT: REFLECTIONS OF A STATE COMMISSIONER OF LABOR

By Kevin P. McCabe

How *does revamping workforce development systems happen? It happens because the people in charge collaborate with local experts, theoreticians, and other politicians. In this chapter former New Jersey Labor Commissioner Kevin P. McCabe presents a comprehensive overview in which he discusses his view of the reorganization of New Jersey workforce services. He argues that the New Jersey experience illustrates how collaboration and an openness to new technology can increase flexibility and help the working poor. This chapter serves as a broad overview of former Commissioner McCabe's informed insights and experiences in consolidating workforce development policy so that it becomes a state priority. For interested read-ers the specifics of the reorganization process are articulated in greater detail in a companion book,* Not Just Getting By: Implementing Innovative Thinking in Government and Workforce Development *(2005).*

"The best welfare program in the world is a job" was a line often cited by Governor James E. McGreevey. In the new knowledge-based economy where downsizing and outsourcing are persistent threats, I would take the Governor's sentiments a step further: that the best welfare program is a *good paying* job. Raised in a blue-collar labor union household my father, who was an electrician by trade and a foreman on the railroad, and my mother, who returned to paid work after raising five kids for twenty years, ensured that work was a given in our household. My parents got up early, worked hard, and provided for my siblings and me. It was not without its tough moments but my parents always persevered and now have retired successfully and spend their time babysitting for the grandchildren!

However, with job loss, dislocation, and most important, skills erosion all as modern facts of life today, it is less common to have the job trajectory that my parents did decades ago. I believe that consistency in today's job market has been replaced by vulnerability. Therefore, the Governor's sentiments really resonated with me when I was first appointed to office in January of 2002. Unfortunately, when I entered office I encountered a bureaucracy that did not subscribe to the market driven economic realities of today's economy. Rather, it was too often engaged in activities that were counterproductive to helping individuals achieve economic self-sufficiency. First, many individuals believed that welfare was a solution to poverty.[1] Second, the intrinsic structure of the bureaucracy too often penalized, rather than rewarded, those who wanted to work and/or obtain more education. Indeed, the system appeared to not help individuals, in particular low-wage workers, gain the tools and resources they needed to achieve economic self-sufficiency.

There needed to be a substantial change in the workforce delivery system. It was clear to many of us that the time had come for changes in the way New Jersey workforce services were conceptualized, prioritized, and delivered.[2] Central to this initiative was the promotion and support of a lifelong learning system that not only positioned workforce development as a major state priority but articulated the importance of providing training and education to *all* workers. Further, we recognized that workforce development indeed is economic development and does not end at job placement. As such in 2002–2004, New Jersey experienced the largest transfer of programs and funding sources from one or more agencies to another in its history.[3] The purpose of this reorganization was quite simple—it sought to provide a seamless system to connect dislocated and low-wage workers with the social supports, job information, and educational opportunities to improve their lives. Implicit in this was the need for innovative programs that provide demand-driven training to low-wage workers. In consolidating and reorganizing workforce development, I argue that this paradigm shift serves to support new and innovative programs, such as using online learning to deliver skills training, that take into account the needs of the working poor and other constituent groups of the workforce system.

As the individual who was primarily responsible to shepherd this initiative, I experienced government change at three critical stages of development. First, I saw how the status quo was not meeting the needs of the citizenry. Second, I experienced the frustration of trying to move decades of government thinking into new directions. Third, we as a Department felt the sense of accomplishment knowing that change occurred for the good of those who needed it: the unemployed, the underemployed, the disadvantaged, and the despondent.

It is my goal to present an overall framework that I believe is effective in delivering education and training to our citizenry based on my experiences in the workforce development field. This section will be an honest portrayal of an almost two year exercise in understanding the nuances of a workforce system that is resistant to the basic notion that change can achieve the greater good. Following this chapter, I will return with Mary Gatta to analytically discuss a vision of workforce development based on each of our expertise in the field that will help low-wage workers attain the skills and education to improve their lives.

IDENTIFYING THE WORKFORCE CHALLENGE IN NEW JERSEY

It was clear that if we were to embark on this ambitious project we needed to get a clear understanding of how the New Jersey workforce system operated. In 2001 the New Jersey State Employment and Training Commission[4] (SETC) issued the policy paper, *New Jersey in Transition: The Crisis of the Workforce*, which capsulated the State of New Jersey's workforce and its ability to address the needs of both workers and employers. Not surprisingly, the major finding of this report was that the workforce development system needed to be reorganized to better deliver services to the labor force and businesses. To reach this conclusion the report outlined the logic of the existing system, noting that education in New Jersey (and indeed the United States) is a triad consisting of the K to 12 system, the higher education system, and the workforce investment system. This third vector of the educational framework—the workforce investment system—comprises a varied constituency group including, among others, the adult population, incumbent workers, high school dropouts, welfare recipients, and immigrants. The key point was that while the K–12 and the higher education systems deliver educational services to the constituent groups of the work-force investment system, their primary mission was not workforce quality. This disjuncture proved alarming to the health of the state's workforce.

The report further noted that compounding this is that the workforce investment system, unlike the K–12 and higher education system, lacks the status, funding, public support, and priority at the state level. As key senior staff member told me:

> The Labor Department is essentially a federal creation. [New Jersey Depart-ment of Labor] did a summary of all this, I remember it was more than 85 percent of Labor's money comes from the federal government and therefore by the very nature of what it does, unemployment insurance, workforce train-ing, is not a state priority because it's not in the state budget.

Further complicating the matter is that numerous state departments and agencies share the responsibility for administering programs and services for the workforce investment system including State Departments of Labor, Education, Human Services, Community Affairs, and the State Commissions of Higher Education, Juvenile Justice, Commerce, and Eco-nomic Growth. These organizations each have distinctive funding streams, missions, staffs, performance measures, and structures despite the fact that they are serving constituency groups within the same population. The dis-parate workforce development programs and services within state govern-ment were unable to effectively meet the needs of the existing, future, and displaced workforce. Moreover, resources were underutilized due to the lack of coordination between the agencies. A high-level staff member in the New Jersey Department of Labor and Workforce Development graphically demonstrated this point.

> [I learned that] that 30 percent of the welfare population can go to school for up to a year into occupational training before they went into a job. But because the welfare department was so concerned and driven by their partic-ipation rates anybody that was work ready they just put them into employ-ment . . . as a result the program was highly underutilized.

Based on such findings the policy recommendation that emerged from the SETC's report was to transform the New Jersey Department of Labor into the New Jersey Department of Labor and Workforce Development. The proposed new department would be responsible for the integration of the service delivery provided by all workforce funding streams.[5] In the existing system, the workforce programs were spread among half a dozen departments and administered in over twenty separate divisions of those departments. The mission of this consolidated department would be to implement the policies developed under the broad authority of the Governor. Further, the report noted that even more important then consolidating programs into one department is to build a management infrastructure to develop strategies to ensure the smooth integration of these programs. The goal of this endeavor was to build a more unified workforce development system that views "workforce development no longer as an extension of social welfare policy, but as an essential part of a state's economic growth strategy" (Ganzglass, Jensen, Ridley, Simon, and Thompson, 2001).

This proved to be a daunting task, in which clear visions of workforce development were necessary. The following sections represent a broad overview of how this consolidation occurred and how the vision of workforce development was rethought to better attend to the needs of all workers.

TRANSITION TO STATE GOVERNMENT

McGreevey appointed my predecessor and one of my mentors, Albert Kroll to the position of Commissioner of Labor in January of 2002. I was appointed Deputy Commissioner and together we spearheaded the State Department of Labor's transition team.[6] During this stage it was our task to interview the departmental leadership to learn about its ongoing projects and to prepare a report for the Governor. Our charge was not only to understand these points but also, and most important, determine how to interweave these projects with the priorities of the incoming McGreevey administration. Looking back it is ironic that while we confronted a number of complex issues and topics we barely recognized the need to review how the state was delivering "to work" activities[7] and training to the unemployed and unskilled incumbent workers.

During the transition we received an education in the structure of the current One-Stop delivery system and the Workforce Investment Boards. The prior leadership of the State Department of Labor told us that since the inception of the Workforce Investment Act (WIA) of 1998 the Department severely lost oversight of the local Workforce Investment Boards

(WIBs). Indeed there was a lack of a coordinated and cohesive vision for the local One-Stop Career Centers, making it difficult to deliver services to individuals in ways that were effective. I equated them to sailboats without wind in the middle of a lake without a ripple of a wave.

As a matter of fact a senior member of the former department wished us "good luck at trying to get the WIBs to work with you. They are all driven by the local politicians. It is too political to deal with them." At the end of his "brave manifestation" I immediately questioned him as to which organization funded the locals WIBs. He replied, "The State Department of Labor does, but that it really is just a pass through." In our minds that was unacceptable and set the stage for what was to become the beginning of a culture change that was desperately needed to occur between the walls and minds of the New Jersey Department of Labor.

GETTING TO WORK: THE RIGHT PERSONNEL FOR THE RIGHT JOB

I have often said to many audiences that when we took office on January 15, 2002, "we did not just wake up and decide that we wanted to induce a multi-million dollar seismic shift that would register a nine on the bureaucratic Richter scale." Such a decision, without developing a thoughtful and coherent blueprint, would have killed the idea before it ever begun. As such, the planning process was pivotal.

First and foremost was to sit down with Assistant Commissioners.[8] As is the case with most new administrations personnel changes where requested of each department. We realized that the Department had a core of Assistant Commissioners and senior staff overseeing each of the program areas whose length of service collectively totaled roughly over 120 years. Of course there were changes that needed to be made, but that core group of Assistant Commissioners and senior staff were instrumental to the anticipated successful reorganizing of the Department. They provided a coherent history of the Department's functions as well as detailed expert knowledge in key areas. As Kroll, the former Commissioner of Labor used to say to me when we disagreed on a certain personnel changes, "what do you know about disability insurance?" His point was that he and I certainly were far from experts in the minutia of the Department and needed the experience of those who "know."

Reflecting on the course of this process, there were several critical periods that enabled us to reorganize workforce development. Addressing the personnel issues within the Department of was one of those critical periods. If we were to pursue this enormous task of reorganizing the workforce development system without first addressing our own problems we would have exposed our own flaws and been vulnerable to failure. Therefore, we reviewed our senior staff and began to make the proper adjustments.[9] Inevitably there were some minor changes to the senior staff. However the real impact changes came within the program areas that directly affected the impending reorganization.

Growing up in an Irish Catholic family I was often told you do not bring the problems within the family to the outside. Simply put, we needed to reorganize our own house before we reorganized the workforce development system. While leadership through senior staff was in place, the way the Department was structured at certain points proved disconcerting. It was quite evident from the first few weeks some New Jersey Department of Labor divisions did not have the necessary staff to support what would be a difficult and contentious battle to reorganize workforce development services. We needed to significantly reorganize the current structure so that staffers were held accountable for work they were committed to and responsible for. To do so we reorganized the Department's structure so that the work was task specific with a clear understanding of each division's responsibilities. By shifting some other existing personnel and redrawing the organizational structure we opened up new placements and were able to bring in qualified individuals.

This was accomplished through various means. We felt that to ensure the viability of the reorganization of workforce development services we needed to recruit seasoned individuals who had served in the One-Stop Career Center locales and who had a clear understanding of the intricacies and the nuances of the day-to-day programs. We understood that to be able to sit at the table with our sister agencies we could not be outmaneuvered. We needed to have individuals who possessed specific expertise on local and state issues representing the Department of Labor. To that purpose we hired into the Department One-Stop Career Center staff to aid the reorganization process. In doing so we accomplished two goals. First, we had the top practitioners in the field working in the Department of Labor for the greater good of the clients in the state. Second, we were able to have those who knew best helping us navigate the bureaucratic waters that we feared could sink the reorganization during negotiations.

THE GLOBAL IS LOCAL: THE WORKFORCE INVESTMENT BOARDS

Once we placed key staff in place we knew it was important to get a handle on whether the WIBs were accomplishing their mandate and how we may assist them. While we were ensuring key staff was in place, we encountered another critical period during the important planning period. As I noted earlier, it was clearly articulated to us early during our transition meeting that the WIBs were autonomous and engineers of their own trains. While we were beginning to engage the Department leadership into the notion of consolidating the "to-work" activities, I worked closely with key senior staff of the Department to seriously grapple with ways to improve the manner the local WIBs delivered services to the client.[10] We agreed that the local One-Stop Career Centers needed to become a truly integrated clearinghouse of services, similar to the way WIA had intended. However, we first had to take care of our own internal issues before we could engage the external stakeholders, as the Department itself was fractured by its own silos. Indeed, since coming to Trenton,[11] I learned more words and catchphrases than I needed to describe how bureaucracies function including: silos, boxes, out of the box, cultures, mindsets, and history. Quite frankly, I interpreted them as just weak synonyms for ineffectiveness, and saw it as just further evidence for rethinking workforce development systems.

One of our early concerns was that the workforce development system was not working as effectively as it should because individuals were not willing to address the issues of the WIBs because of local political reasons. I knew we were approaching an opportunity to address this issue. To do so, we conducted surveys of each WIB and "graded" them,[12] without prejudice, based on the criteria set forth by WIA. After months of surveying the local One-Stop Career Centers our most significant discovery was the absence of a uniform structure of a One-Stop Career Center in the state.[13] In other words, although we agreed that there needed to be local flexibility in the planning of One-Stop Career Centers, we maintained that there needed to be a consistent blueprint to serve the needs of the local. After all, the One-Stops were the vehicles by which training was to be delivered throughout the state. It was our contention that whether an individual is seeking service in one of our northern urban areas or southern rural areas, the basic services should be available in all areas.

To address this we spent many months meeting with each individual WIB directors, local leadership, and appropriate staff. The purpose of these meetings was to begin serious relationship building and developing an open, honest, and ongoing dialogue with the WIBs. In addition, it allowed us to set our agenda and to collaboratively implement the changes that were necessary to create a better system that truly served the clients. Paramount on our list was the true integration of the local One-Stop Career Centers. From the data we reviewed and the personal trips we made to the Centers we discovered that it was a fractured system. It was frustrating for us to imagine how a twenty-year employee and father of two who had just been laid off from the local plant would have to go to several different locations just to obtain the training he needed and deserved to get back into the job market. Or how a single working poor mother who only wanted to improve her abilities to strengthen and promote herself would have to get on two different busses to go to multiple "One" Stop Career Centers to try to get access to education and training. Indeed, the term "One Stop" in certain parts of the state was actually an embarrassing oxymoron not serving individuals needs.[14]

After we began meeting with the WIBs and local leadership I realized that these meetings were becoming like a therapy session. It was almost like a cleansing process that forced us to not only articulate our concerns with their performance but it was the first time that we heard what the department was doing wrong. This points to the importance of open communication and dialogue in policy formation. During these meetings we agreed to review and address their concerns as well as work with them on issues that they felt they could not address alone. Not only did we agree in theory but for the first time we mandated that both parties collaborate to construct goals and objectives which were to be completed by an aggressive, yet realistic timetable. (It was clear that we wanted this done sooner rather than later.) This allowed us to develop credibility with the locals that together we could actually produce a change for the right reasons—those that were for the good of the client. Over a two year period we not only truly integrated the One-Stop Career Centers[15] but we worked with them to open within the One-Stop Career Centers other important amenities such as child drop-off centers, literacy labs, business resource centers, and a card scan system for tracking clients.

To be clear, this did not become a utopia. As long as government exists there will always be differences and disagreements. However, the fact that there were discussions taking place at all was a victory unto itself. Once again, we had to build credibility within the WIB community to develop real and lasting relationships. Even though we did not want to hear about

the local domain and the political issues with this process we never forgot
Tip O'Neill's basic, yet profound, statement: "All politics are local."

LEADERSHIP

There is no stronger attribute or more powerful component of government
than leadership. I define a leader as the person who is willing to take a risk
to try to affect change and accept the consequences of their actions
whether they are good or bad. Two different quotes about leadership have
encapsulated my leadership strategy throughout my career. The first was
often recited by Governor McGreevey as he noted, "I don't need to be
liked. I just want to be to be respected." Quite simply, leaders often have
to make the unpopular decisions. In addition, an "old school" labor leader
who was not afraid to speak his mind, usually peppered with several four
letter words, offered this piece of advice on being a leader. He told me that
"If the person in front of you doesn't move, go the f°°° around them."

The need for leadership at the highest levels of government was evidenced in discussions I had with former senior staff from previous administrations. A former Commissioner of another department told us that there
was quite a history of trying to locate all the "to work" activities under the
auspices of the New Jersey Department of Labor. He told us that even
though conceptually he thought the idea made practical sense he indicated
that it never really registered on the state's radar screen. When we questioned him as to why, he replied with just one word: leadership, or more
aptly, a lack thereof. He told us that for the past twenty years while people
talked about consolidating workforce development programs, he knew that
if there was not a clear mandate from the Governor, on record, in a public
forum then the bureaucratic structure would never let it happen. At that
moment it dawned on me that we speak about the bureaucracy almost as if
we were talking about a creature in a horror film. A faceless beast, that if
one is left vulnerable, it will eat you up without remorse. To slay this beast
it will not take a knight on a white horse or a superhero but someone willing
to demonstrate leadership.

Yet one does not need just one leader, but a collaborative group that is
willing to work together to move forward an initiative. To that purpose I
found that there are three individuals that that were instrumental to the
development, the evolution, and the inevitable success of the reorganiza-

tion of the workforce development system. I label them as the visionary, the general, and the champion for rethinking the way we deliver services to the most important constituency in the state: the worker. I believe that such individuals are vital to move decades-old bureaucracies and essentially change the way a state delivers its workforce training.

The three individuals I am referring to are SETC Chairman John Heldrich,[16] whom I call the "visionary"; former Commissioner of Labor Albert Kroll,[17] whom I term the "general"; and Governor James E. McGreevey, whom I refer to as the "champion." These leaders shared a common goal that emerged from the various positions and perspectives of their lives. They represented business, the public sector, and the political leadership. Indeed, I would argue that for this to be successful one must assemble a team consisting of individuals who represents each of these components. A single individual could not make this happen alone; collaborative leadership is necessary.

The visionary is able to present a large blueprint that moves individuals' thinking beyond the confines of traditional understanding. This needs to be someone who is senior level and well respected, so that he/she can excite the passions in others. The general is the individual who is able to effectively bring together the key stakeholders, interpret the plan into a practical fashion, and mobilize others to execute the plan. Finally, the champion is the public face for the policy change. He/she must be a well-known figure who is able to provide the issue with high level of visibility. The champion, as a powerful opinion leader, brings credibility to the project with his/her stamp of approval. In addition, this "trifecta" of leaders also shared common traits that were essential to the success of reorganizing a state workforce development system. Each possessed a genuine passion for improving the economic self-sufficiency of others, and shared a common vision on how to achieve it. Also, each had a personal investment and commitment to see the reorganization of the workforce development system to its completion. Finally, each valued the expertise not only of each other but also that of individuals inside and outside of the state bureaucracy and turned to them for advice and support throughout this process.

PUBLIC FORUMS AND A MANDATE

When we discussed with others that the Governor was in agreement with the reorganization there was strong skepticism from inside and outside state government. Our sister agencies did not blink an eye and the public stakeholders did not waste their energy preparing to mount an opposition campaign. However, three critical periods occurred that served to demonstrate the state's commitment, and perhaps most important, each event was executed in the public arena.

At this point we had the necessary personnel in place and had met with the Governor's staff to ensure they understood what we were trying to accomplish. During this period, the SETC was preparing for its annual One-Stop Career Conference.[18] For weeks the Executive Director had asked me to petition the Governor's office to have the conference placed on his schedule and for him to address the audience. Since all the principal partners and members of the WIBs and One-Stop community participated in this conference we believed that it would be the right time to launch the "trial balloon." It seemed quite simple, but strategic—just have the Governor include in his speech a statement alluding to the need to restructure and rethink the way we deliver workforce services. We were able to persuade the Governor's Office of this idea and secure the Governor for the conference. Simultaneously, two other important moments were taking shape.

The Chair of the State Senate Labor Committee asked the Department for our priorities for the upcoming year and to present them at a public hearing. Of course, this was our opportunity to present to the Committee our idea to reorganize workforce development services and, with the support and encouragement of the Governor's office, we would have our sister agencies with us to present a united front. We worked with both the staff of the committee and the Governor's office to educate all the interested parties. During this same period we met with key stakeholders in the labor movement, business, and education to gain momentum and to demonstrate public strength in preparation for the hearing.

Perhaps one of the most politically astute moves occurred during the testimony provided by key leaders, including Henry Plotkin, the Executive Director of the SETC; Heldrich; and Kroll at the Senate Labor Committee hearing. The Senate Committee asked us to set forth a timetable when a preliminary plan of the reorganization would be completed. Keenly, Kroll replied "by the end of the calendar year." This translated into a forty-five day time period. The Chairman of the Committee was taken by surprise at the aggressive response set forth by the Department. More important, it put our sister agencies and our own staff on notice.

This set the tone that the time for dialogue was over, and it was now time to begin to act.

Meanwhile, we were developing another key support group as we were preparing for the conferences and the hearings, that of the Governor's staff. While it is necessary to have the Governor and his Chief Operating Officers committed, I found it was equally important to mobilize the Governor's policy and message staff. They were intrigued that the Governor, who was raised in a working-class town and household, would be tackling issues pertaining to the needs of everyday workers. Bringing in the "middle" level staff was significant as we were now gaining more strength in broadening the circle in the Governor's office.

Then a simple phone call to my office provided another significant benchmark. The Governor's Deputy Chief of Staff called me to inform us that the Governor's office wanted to do a "Workforce Summit." He asked for the Department to partner with the State Employment and Training Commission and an academic research organization to design and implement a summit that would include academia, labor unions, businesses (large and small), elected leaders, state officials, community based organizations, and nonprofits. To us there could not have been a better message to send than that these issues were being brought to the policy forefront. This time the Governor was not just going to mention the initiative in a speech before a particular constituency in a hotel meeting room. Indeed, the whole conference was focused on what we had been discussing and preparing for over the past year. The Governor announced, with the press present and in front of over five hundred people, that the Department of Labor would not only serve as the lead agency for all of the workforce programs but to underscore these efforts, the Department would be renamed at the conclusion of the reorganization to the Department of Labor and Workforce Development. Now we had to get to work.

REORGANIZATION

Even though there was a tremendous amount of work and sweat equity that went into the preparation to reorganize workforce development services, the hard part was about to begin. There are three key components that guided the entire reorganization—a flexible structure, communication, and planning. Although these three concepts may appear to be quite simple, they were both important to its success.

As I noted earlier leadership plays a key role in formulating and maintaining a solid structure. We needed to develop a working committee consisting of individuals representing the three participating state departments (Labor, Education, and Human Services) that would facilitate the creation of the new workforce development system. The main objective of this committee was to create a reorganization plan that would be submitted to the Governor for him to deliver to the legislature. The structure of the committee needed to be designed so it forced the parties to confront each other, to meet specific deadlines and hold individual agencies accountable. As such, it required collaboration and communication. The New Jersey Department of Labor was to take the lead on this endeavor. This was an essential point because it demonstrated an "employment and skills development" mindset that would guide policy and programs.

The structure of this committee consisted of decisionmakers that could make strong recommendations to their respective Commissioners, along with the Attorney General's office. I was asked to spearhead this committee and felt this was an opportunity for the Department to effect the substantial change needed to provide what we had prepared for, without interference from the bureaucracy itself. The Governor's mandate and the structure we created helped to emasculate the bureaucracy that for years had stood for the status quo.

A main objective of this committee was to build partnerships across bureaucratic divides. In reality, this translated into a considerable amount of work, most notably, reviewing and interpreting the legal regulations, personnel responsibilities, existing educational vendors, fiscal issues, and legislative requirements. Our mandate was to not only review this data but to improve the existing system. Out of these dialogues came three important principles that guided the reorganization of workforce services—the need for flexibility, communication, and planning.

Flexibility

The previous workforce system was not flexible for the unemployed worker, the low-wage worker, or the employer. I contend that flexibility is imperative to delivering services to all constituent groups. While the word "flexibility" is used often in state government it is seldom sufficiently conceptualized. We toss the word "flexibility" around in state government chambers readily and yet it has become empty rhetoric. Flexibility is an essential part of daily life for the employer and the employee. For example, we had discussions with a business owner who told us that he actually had to hire a staff member to track the grants that he received from the state. Even more disconcerting is that since unemployment insurance was not originally part of the One-Stop System,[19] when an individual picked up his/her check, there was not a seamless way for she/he to simultaneously attain job market information or training. The old system saw unemployment offices while we envisioned career centers.

In order to make the system more flexible we recommended that all "to work" programs be consolidated into the One-Stop Career System. This allowed for individuals (either dislocated workers, low-wage workers, and employers) to connect with jobs, education, and training. Central to this is the idea that the system must evolve with the demands of the ever-changing economy. To accomplish this, it is necessary to understand the demographics of local areas both in terms of the labor force composition and the demand of the employment sector. In this way the workforce system can respond to the needs of both labor force members and employers.

Flexibility then is directly tied to effective responsiveness to both workers and employers. Online learning programs, along with other innovative forms of education and training help to improve flexibility by providing not only opportunities as to where and when individuals can take classes but also greater customer choice in the types of training available. If the public sector collaborates with educational vendors, employers, and community colleges the available training opportunities online will outpace the courses that are available in traditional classroom settings. By using distance learning methods we can provide greater access to a variety of skills training programs to larger numbers of workers. In addition, we can better respond to the changing economy as we can create more individualized employment plans that are better tied to demand jobs in the local area. So we can bring the best training programs to individuals regardless of location.

Communication

Throughout this process I have alluded to collaborations. Let me be frank, the fiefdoms endemic to state government, along with a lack of understanding of organizational histories and the need to maintain external relationships with stakeholders, make communication and collaboration a difficult venture and, indeed, made this process labor intensive. It is important to reiterate that change (good or bad) is extremely difficult. Interestingly, the reason for the difficulty is because those who have a vested interest become complacent and comfortable with a system they know, and are concerned about losing their place with what they perceive to be an unknown. Therefore, it was important that we constructed a marketing plan aimed at not just selling this idea to the stakeholders but, in fact, build relationships to develop credibility. For years the Department was perceived as the state's largest public insurance company, so the idea of a bureaucracy of this nature taking the lead on an innovative idea was foreign to those that were part of the old system.

The initial step then was to develop open communication with the various stakeholders and interested parities. This was accomplished by first communicating a clear vision of the end goal to all the interested parities. We needed to ensure that the stakeholders would have a real voice in restructuring the workforce system. In doing so, they needed to feel ownership of the process. We held a series of meetings at the State Department with the three agencies and all the relevant stakeholders to ascertain their needs and concerns regarding the workforce system. Most important, it was an opportunity for the groups to share their concerns and issues, and for us to collaboratively work to resolve them.

In addition to open communication with key agencies and stakeholders, we also have to develop communication with legislators, the press, and nontraditional alliances such as the business and education associations. These collaborations were important because as we were trying to reinvent a better form of workforce services, at the same time we were trying to reinvent the image of the Department. This was important because we needed to develop credibility in the workforce development system, so that individuals would avail themselves of it.

Planning

When I first embarked on the reorganization I failed to recognize what was to be the most important component of the entire process—planning. I am not referring to the planning of the internal and political tactics to mobilize will. I am referring to the underrated local planning that was initiated and implemented by the SETC. When the SETC Executive Director approached me about this concept I told him that planning would be his domain and then did not give much thought to the subject. However, my nonchalance toward planning was short-lived. I soon recognized that in order for a planning process to be taken seriously, top leadership must endorse it. As I alluded to earlier, I recalled that it was in fact the mandate from Kroll and I that we finally forced the locals to immediately address the issue of designing true "One" Stop Career Centers. In other words, we committed the support necessary to ensure that the planning process would be a priority for the remainder of the reorganization.

After gaining a better understanding of this issue it was an easy decision for us when the SETC suggested that the planning process begin with a retreat. The retreat would include all the relevant staff of each local WIBs. There would be a two-way dialogue between the state and the locals. By now I would imagine that the reader is saying to himself/herself that in state government all you have are a series of meetings, retreats, and summits. This is true. However, it was these venues that served as the impetus to promote and force communication and flexibility.

I used to say at our meeting with the local WIBs that "the minute the planning process ceases to continue is the minute the reorganization ceases to work." My point was that this initiative was not going to end the moment we introduced the reorganization or when the Governor signed the legislation. In fact, I would maintain that the reason that most initiatives, primarily in workforce development, fail is due to the overall lack of vision, communication, and flexibility necessary to succeed.

Planning inherently forces nontraditional or reluctant partners to sit down and to communicate with each other. More important, it forces these entities to sometimes enter brutally honest discussions that they would not even entertain before. Collaborative planning tears down the walls of ignorance and opens doors to the hallways of progressive and productive thinking. We discovered that the locals, albeit reluctant to allow the state to suggest ideas that encroached on their turf, needed guidance and best practices from the state and their colleagues.

What is exciting about this planning process is that it provides for flexibility with regard to the local and regional economic markets. Thereby a region and/or state will not be caught flat-footed when inevitability, as we have historically seen, the local economic markets change. For example, as the manufacturing base of many cities eroded there was a lack of infrastructure and long-term planning to fill the economic void that was left behind. The recent expansion of Atlantic City's gaming and hotel industry all but dictates that the local multi-county training programs incorporate the gaming and hospitality industry. The public sector needs to be cognizant of such issues as specific industries become anchors of the local economic region.

As is evident, planning must not only serve as a short-term fix but, in fact, it must be the long-term connection bringing together all the relevant partners to ensure that the workforce development system is not caught behind the market driven economy. The planning process is an evolving process. During this evolution, as I have witnessed firsthand, planning was the catalyst for both communication and the construct of a flexible, rationale local plan.

Conclusion: Reorganizing for the Worker

As I demonstrated, workforce development theory and practice must be a coherent system. Throughout the process of reorganizing workforce development we developed several practices that I believe will best serve workforce development in the twenty-first century. We were aware that "simply" reorganizing the state's workforce services would not serve as the end solution to workforce training's ills. However, what may be most important was recognizing that we could no longer accept the status quo if we wish to sustain a strong workforce and economy. It is my contention that if it were not for the administration's priority, along with the insistence and perseverance of the leadership, the online learning program for single working poor mothers would neither have been successful nor even contemplated as a pilot program. The State's commitment to organizing workforce development services in ways that are flexible and focus on the needs of workers was able to bring to the forefront the challenges that working poor women (among other groups) confront in attaining skills and education and forced us to develop programs to address them. This was evidenced through the communication with key stakeholder groups, as we had to confront the realization that simply being employed does not guarantee self-sufficiency. In today's socioeconomic climate the public sector's complacency will only continue to enable dependency. Government must take an active role to assist in promoting financial independence. I have often spoke of the need for collaboration, and I believe that it is just as important to understand that collaboration also has to be developed between government and the individual. However, it is our job, as appointed policy officials, not to turn a blind eye to the barriers that confront low-wage earners in our community. Indeed, it is by acknowledging them and addressing them head-on that we can affect positive change.

NOTES

1. It is important to note that I believe that welfare policy is critical to help provide individuals with the social supports and assistance that they need to support themselves and their dependents.

2. This is not intended to be an endorsement of the particular way that New Jersey reorganized, but instead as a first-hand insider account that can be treated as a case study of New Jersey's experience in reorganizing its workforce development system to better attend to the education and training needs of all workers.

3. New Jersey is not the only state in which such a reorganization of workforce development occurred. Other states such as Michigan, Indiana, Louisiana, Pennsylvania, and Utah have engaged in similar reorganizations. See Ganzglass, Jensen, Ridley, Simon, and Thompson (2001) for an extended discussion.

4. The State Employment and Training Commission was established by state legislation in 1989 to be a bipartisan Commission to address the needs of meeting the challenge of the workforce investment system for New Jersey. More recently, the SETC has been designated the State Workforce Investment Board through the federal Workforce Investment Act.

5. Even though the SETC report recommended that all five of the state departments be consolidated, the actual reorganization consisted of only three departments.

6. The transition team is the committee selected by the Governor-elect's office to undertake all reviews and recommendations pertaining to the daily functions of a state department to the Governor.

7. The "to work" activities include all the programs that have been earmarked for training, continuing education, postsecondary, and adult education.

8. In the organization chart in the Department of Labor an Assistant Commissioner oversees the daily operations of a particular program area within the Department and reports directly to the Deputy Commissioner.

9. It is interesting to note that simultaneously we were also engaged in other high profile issues. One of those initiatives I refer to as my "Class A minor league training" to what would eventually be the major leagues with the "to work" reorganization. For many years the department oversaw the daily operations of boiler vessels and asbestos licensing and enforcement. Under a previous administration those operations were transferred to another state department and we planned to have them returned to the New Jersey Department of Labor.

When we first entered into discussions with our sister agency I sat in on the initial meeting and allowed some of our appropriate senior staff the ability to negotiate, make decisions, and report back to me. After a few months we signed an interagency agreement and assumed the responsibilities the New Jersey Department of Labor once had. However, after a few weeks our staff uncovered that we had assumed these responsibilities without the knowledge that there were over six thousand boiler vessels that were unaccounted for in the entire state. This meant that there were six thousand boilers in stores, laundromats, schools, buildings, and tenements that either had not been inspected or that there was no record of any inspection. Essentially neither our staff nor our sister agency provided me with this key information, and I realized I needed to be more proactive and create a structure that would have forced both entities to either divulge the appropriate information or force us to ask the appropriate questions. From that point on we put in a structure for both external and internal meetings that would hopefully diminish the chances of repeat occurrence that took place during these negotiations.

10. Client is defined as the individual worker and the employer.

11. The state capital of New Jersey, where the state offices are located.

12. The grading consisted of meeting the goals and measurables set forth in the federal legislation.

13. It is important to note that there are eighteen WIB's throughout the state of New Jersey. There are three WIBs that have combined counties and there are two cities that have their own.

14. An example of this hodgepodge was a county that had in one city, two different One-Stop Career Centers. They had a county and municipal One-Stop both of which were within blocks of each other.

15. During the writing of this book there were continued successful openings of truly integrated One-Stop Career Centers in various parts of the state.

16. A former long-time executive at Johnson & Johnson Pharmaceutical, who has advocated for workforce development policies for decades in New Jersey.

17. Before being appointed Commissioner of the Department of Labor, Albert Kroll was a labor attorney practicing for thirty years.

18. The One-Stop Career Conference is an annual conference that showcases employment and training programs throughout the state and brought awareness of key workforce development state initiatives.

19. A mandated part of the reorganization was the inclusion of unemployment insurance in the One-Stop System.

6

CONCLUDING REMARKS: DEVELOPING AN AGENDA FOR WORKFORCE DEVELOPMENT AND LOW-WAGE WORKERS

Policymakers and policy researchers can collaborate to develop and implement workforce development agendas that attend to the needs of low-wage workers. In this concluding chapter we share a conversation in which former Commissioner McCabe and I suggest a comprehensive agenda of workforce development and demonstrate the important perspectives social scientists and policymakers bring to bear in these discussions.

Mary Gatta: Kevin, one of the interesting things that drew me to the New Jersey online learning project was that it created a training program for individuals who typically fall through the cracks of our workforce system. These are low-wage workers, and—as we saw in the demographics—these women earned about $18,000 a year. So that made them slightly above minimum wage workers. This program attended to the fact that simply working and making minimum wage or slightly above it, is not enough to get by. It acknowledged that you have to invest in your human capital, but you have to do it in a way that attends to workers' needs.

Kevin McCabe: The reason why we got involved—and I say we because we need to give credit where credit is due—my predecessor, Al Kroll, jumped on this early because he saw it as an opportunity. We knew that we needed to get the reorganization of workforce services done, but this project actually worked well because it was easy to fit in, even though we were reorganizing. Secondly, and perhaps most importantly, is that my predecessor came from a working poor family out of Philadelphia, and he saw this as an opportunity that he would have liked to have for his working mother. For myself, I would think, the two of us agree that philosophically we thought that this was the right thing to do. It was the right thing to do for people that needed it most.

Mary Gatta: I think related to that is there needs to be passion and commitment on part of the individuals who are implementing the policies and delivering the services.

Kevin McCabe: Passion and commitment all too often gets lost in government and bureaucracy. In this case we were committed about being passionate about the reorganization and the online learning program. We knew that the reorganization needed to get done. As I've said a million times, and I'll say it again, this was not the idea of Kevin McCabe or Al Kroll. This was an idea that went back twenty years. In interviews and conversations that we had it was illustrated to us that people agreed it was not only the right thing to do, it was the most sensible thing to do. We had an antiquated system that wasn't flexible and wasn't meeting the needs of modern twenty-first century workforce development. The online learning program is a modern twenty-first century workforce program. So the two of them blend well, it just made logical sense.

And you need to be committed to a passion when you're dealing in a bureaucracy. If you don't the bureaucracy will eat you up. And this is not to speak ill of anybody, but I just think it's inherent in the system. So you need to show a dedication and perseverance. We were very clear on what our priorities were. We knew that the reorganization was going to be a priority and out of the reorganization came the online learning program. We were committed to getting it done, and we did.

Mary Gatta: What is important is that if you don't get somebody in the top leadership to get excited about it, it doesn't work. So, and that speaks to what you say, you have this bureaucracy, but you need to have somebody who's able to move initiatives forward within the bureaucracy.

Kevin McCabe: If you look back historically at the nation's past initiatives spearheaded by our past leaders, if they didn't have a passion or commitment these great initiatives that took place would not have. Documents such as our Declaration of Independence or our Constitution may never have been written. The successes that Abraham Lincoln accomplished, Teddy Roosevelt, FDR, JFK, and the man on the moon, you can go on and on—and they each had a passion and commitment to an initiative that they wanted to see get done. Now clearly I'm not comparing what we did to any of those initiatives, but this gets back to the argument: if you have leadership that's passionately committed to an issue it will get done regardless of any obstacles.

Mary Gatta: Related to that it's not just leadership at the government end, but there really is a role for academia within the public sector.

Kevin McCabe: We utilized the Center for Women and Work to be the oversight for the online learning program. And the rationale for that is that you want those who know, and those with the expertise, like yourself, to assist. On any major initiative if you do not utilize the resources afforded to you, you are only hurting yourself and the client you are trying to serve. I think an outgrowth of the partnership that we developed between the Department of Labor and academia allowed us to develop a broader coalition, because other entities saw for the first time in a long time—and this is what people told me in the Department who have been there for twenty, twenty-five years—that the Department of Labor was able to take the lead on a major initiative. In doing so those other entities—stakeholders if you will—saw that we were willing to work with academia, which is a nontraditional partner. Therefore, we were able to build up credibility with other interested parties who historically held a suspicious eye toward the Department.

Mary Gatta: Well, historically there has been a distrust of the government from academia and vice versa. And I think there's some disdain on both ends. So to me what is really important is that in this example we were able to collaborate and form coalitions, and each entity maintained its perspectives. No one was subsumed in somebody else's perspectives.

Kevin McCabe: Identity and identifying an individual's issues are very important.

Mary Gatta: And respect. I think respect is important too in this. Respect helped to ensure that everybody was able to—or each entity was able to—

maintain its identity and its mission. For example, the Center for Women and Work's mission, as an academic entity, is to inform policies, it's not to institute them and it's not to run training programs. In informing policies we bring a perspective into workforce development that takes into account gender and women's experiences. So if we can feed that into policy, that's something that's important.

Kevin McCabe: Maybe because it's relying on each other's strong points and each other's resources. But allowing entities to continue to maintain their own identities was very important. That's why when we brought in the stakeholders we created a forum that allowed them to formulate, process, and then articulate what their concerns were going to be. Actually it was rather seamless. It was not as contentious as I thought it would've been.

Mary Gatta: A strong point that I think academia brings is a perspective that is much broader than assuming that everything can be pigeonholed in one category. What was significant about the online project was that it acknowledged that women face many demands on their lives. They have their paid shift in the workforce and then their unpaid shift at home. In addition, many of them are working multiple jobs and face childcare demands. So it brought in some of the language and thinking of academia right into the public sector.

Kevin McCabe: Well, I think what we had with the original five WIBs that piloted the online project was a package that needed to be organized. I think what you did Mary was provide the oversight and gave us the recommendations that we could utilize. You provided the best practices. I think that's imperative as we look to move this onto a larger national stage. Other states, institutions, and entities want to know the pitfalls. They certainly don't want to step in a pothole that we already stepped in and bruised an ankle. So if you bring this to them they're going to be reassured that those with the expertise helped craft the model.

Mary Gatta: There are then real ways that academia and government can work together. Building on what you said, it's recognizing that each has it's own expertise. But I think one of the challenges that still exist is that there are many myths about academic researchers in the public sector. Often individuals think that research is separate from practice. And that is not the case. There is a lot of good research that is grounded in lives that can be applied to policies and programs. I think part of what still is a barrier in coalitions is that academics aren't always willing to package their research in a way that it can be user-friendly, and policymakers still sometimes see academia as separate from reality.

Kevin McCabe: I think there is strong hesitation in government to take huge risks. I think academia can serve as a supplement to government and provide trial and error. Academia can assist government by serving as oversight and finding solutions to any problem that may exist during the planning and implementation on any initiative.

Mary Gatta: It is the importance of creating and maintaining partnerships.

Kevin McCabe: I believe it's a process. Partnerships breed collaborations and collaborations breed relationships. Someone just recently told me "Do you know how you really know when you can build a relationship? When you have to work together." And that's how you build relationships. Sometimes they don't always work, but I think you'll find, instead of just the cocktail party banter or the political shtick, it's about actually having to roll up your sleeves and getting into the nuts and bolts of any issue and trying to find solutions to problems jointly.

Mary Gatta: I think that assessment is accurate Kevin. Each partner then not only brings its resources to the table, but as you get to know the entities you develop respect and an understanding of other perspectives. I think that's really critical. It is similar to breaking down any stereotype; you then gain experience and knowledge. I think that there is great potential for a partnership between academia and government on this initiative and other workforce initiatives.

Kevin McCabe: Absolutely. I don't know if the rigid nature of government can keep up with the rapid changes and trends that are taking place in the private sector of the economy. I'm not convinced it can. I think there are changes that need to be made, and academia can do a much better job of keeping up with the trends. Let me give you another example of a collaboration we fostered. We petitioned the SETC and the John J. Heldrich Center at Rutgers University to do a "demand side survey." Our goal was to survey nine employment sectors and hundreds of employers statewide to determine what skills were going to be necessary in five years time. We understood that for New Jersey to remain competitive economically we needed to be ahead of the curve. I do not believe that we, the Department, could have undertaken this task without the collaboration of both academia and the private sector.

Mary Gatta: That is the job of researchers—to document trends and understand what's going on.

Kevin McCabe: Government, specifically the individuals charged with promoting economic opportunities and job growth throughout the state, would probably do themselves a favor by relying on research on workforce development. That should be a natural.

Mary Gatta: To that point I think part of the job of researchers is then to make sure that research is relevant, up to date, and is produced in a usable fashion. Further, researchers need to disseminate their findings to as broad of an audience as possible. In doing so it helps share best practices throughout the country.

Kevin McCabe: Absolutely. In fact, I think the online learning model we utilized in New Jersey should serve as the template nationally. Other states can utilize the model and shape it for their own local issues. As the gap between the rich and the poor continues to widen and as the middle class is getting squeezed, single working poor mothers are grappling with the day-to-day issues that most of us have a tough time comprehending. We recognized this in New Jersey. Hopefully it will allow other states to gain a full perspective of what these individuals are going through and how to develop training programs that will work within their daily lives. Simply put, the online program provides for an innovative and flexible opportunity that helps to address the issues in the twenty-first century society that we live in.

Mary Gatta: I think it's important to know why we picked single working poor mothers. The choice was strategic on two accounts. First, it was because they typically face all the education and work barriers, so if it works with this group its will more than likely work for other groups. You can make that argument. And the other is they are the fastest growing group in poverty.

Kevin McCabe: We as a nation can ill afford to lose any constituency of our society through the existing cracks of our economic foundation. As you have said, single working mothers are the fastest growing segment of poverty. Therefore, to me it just makes sound fiscal sense to provide relatively inexpensive solutions, such as workforce development training, and specifically, the online learning program. These short-term opportunities seem to be more beneficial in the long-term than a woman caring for two children who is on public assistance and costing all of us considerable more in dollars and cents. I also believe, generally speaking, that individuals would rather take advantage of an opportunity to improve themselves and their families as opposed to relying on federal assistance. Simply put, based on my own experiences growing up in a working/middle-class household, I firmly believe a good paying job and skills training allows one to develop a sense of dignity for themselves and their children.

Mary Gatta: Kevin, your point is well taken. You have often suggested investing in the workforce is a significant way to address issues of poverty. To do that you have said that states must frame workforce development as a core economic development strategy. To facilitate this the public sector needs to provide a seamless workforce delivery system, and we must align all workforce programs in a consolidated organization that establishes collaborations with welfare programs, educational entities, community-based programs, labor unions, and other related programs.

Kevin McCabe: I cannot stress it enough that workforce development has to be a state and national priority. Workforce development and retraining is not a "sexy" issue. The way you make it sexy is to have it relate directly to individuals—to help individuals achieve self-sufficiency so that businesses have access to a skilled workforce. There must be a basic understanding that government is willing to commit the resources and all the necessary elements to make sure that if you are laid off, if you are trying to improve your quality of life by improving your status at your current job, if you are seeking training and education, or if you are looking at getting over social hurdles, the resources will be available to the individual.

Mary Gatta: And it's understanding, too, that education—specifically, access to education—needs to be democratized so that everyone can take advantage. And that is what is really promising about the online option. It is a way to really democratize access across many different variables: class, gender, race, disability, age, etc.

Kevin McCabe: The infrastructure of the old workforce system was so convoluted and complex. You know in New Jersey we talked about over twenty different funding sources in five different agencies, and three of them the major ones—Human Services, Education, and Labor, which for the most part were all providing the same services. This would remind one of a very bad DNA sample if you looked at it on paper. What was even more frustrating, and became a convincing argument for us, in addition to being confusing, complex, and convoluted, the system was not flexible. Our system of government and the foundation by which we are going to be providing training has to be as flexible as the global economy.

Mary Gatta: Kevin, let us talk about flexibility in workforce development. There is much research that the labor market continually is changing. With those changes, the skills demanded of workers continue to increase. We know that life-long learning is critical to maintaining and increasing one's earnings and one's career advancement and that is true at all levels. There is a lot of good research that demonstrates this. A high school education is not enough to compete. For many jobs, including those in the service sector you need to know how to interface with technology. So I understand how the work and economy is flexible. The challenge becomes how do you create workforce development systems that also are flexible. Your discussion earlier is heartening because it showed how we could move years of bureaucratic thinking and structures.

Kevin McCabe: You need to tear down barriers, and leadership needs to be creative and innovative in how achieve that goal. What was significant to that point was we framed the issues as collaborations between the employer and the employee. This gets back to my earlier point that I made about undertaking a "demand side study" of identifying future skill needs. Once again I cannot reiterate this point enough: we need to understand all facets of our economy. Therefore it begins by recognizing the future trends and directions that the market will be dictating. And as a result we need to make sure our nation's workforce is as prepared and responsive as is needed.

Mary Gatta: So really then we need to think about the workforce development system as a comprehensive system that has different vectors that do different things, but through the basic structure it really must connect people and organizations to resources that they need.

Kevin McCabe: Right. So it will connect you to training if you need training. It will connect you to jobs if you a need a job. It will connect you to skilled workers if you need to fill labor demands. It will direct you to human service agencies if you have substance dependency issues. It is a holistic approach and that was our goal when we truly co-located the One-Stop Career Centers in New Jersey.

Mary Gatta: So you maintain that the One-Stop Career system has the infrastructure to make this work. These are integrated centers where individuals can access job training and education, along with labor market information, and other services they may need—access to food stamps, childcare, and other social and economic supports.

Kevin McCabe: The One-Stop Career system provides a critical framework. Currently, I do not believe that there is a silver bullet to cure the workforce system. However, I would contend that the programs you mention are all there, yet for a considerable amount of time they had existed separately. The most significant barrier was trying to restructure the bureaucracy within the workforce development system. That is to say, getting the mindset of these different entities to think for the common goal was not an easy task. As I talked about in the previous chapter, this took a lot of work and sweat equity. There needs to be a common vision and commitment at all levels of government to make this happen.

Mary Gatta: Part and parcel to this commitment is not just to be willing to rethink the bureaucratic structures of state government but also to recognize incumbent workers as a group that must be included in the workforce development schema. In regard to low-wage workers we need to develop flexible systems to provide them with education and training, along with work and educational supports that will help them achieve economic self-sufficiency. There are growing groups of individuals who are low-wage workers who not only cannot afford education and training but also have no idea how to go about getting it. There is a significant role for the public sector to play.

Kevin McCabe: Right. Once you create a centralized clearinghouse for employment and training resources that is really just a first step, albeit a large step! You then need to develop a strategy to connect individuals to the resources and, eventually, employers.

Mary Gatta: That is very true, and you need to be flexible in your approach. What was exciting about the online pilot project was that it used technology to find ways to provide women with training and education that attend to the experiences of their lives. By bringing the training to them, be it in their home or their workplace, women were able to take advantage of it in ways that better integrated education with their family and work lives.

Kevin McCabe: To that I think that workforce development is really about economic development. It is providing education and training that is tied to local business needs that individuals can access at different points in their lives. For it to be successful there needs to be not only the educational and job resources available but also the support systems available—childcare, transportation, income supports (such as Earned Income Tax Credit), among others. So we need to begin to bring services to low-wage workers.

Mary Gatta: And in terms of technology now there are a lot of moments. So, if you want to be on top of things, it is about taking advantage of technology. I think that technology is most interesting in that it can increase flexibility. But the fact that the Internet can decrease barriers and can be used creatively for workforce development is what is interesting about the relationship between workforce development and technology. The fact that you can do training on a computer, you're providing training on the technology that is changing the work and skills needed.

Kevin McCabe: Right, and we're doing that now for those who are in their twenties, thirties, forties, whomever. But if children in grade school don't encounter this as soon as they possibly can we will lose our competitive edge as a nation. I didn't have that training in grade school on computers. I don't know if you did but we really didn't.

Mary Gatta: We were the Commodore #64 computer generation.

Kevin McCabe: Yeah, the Commodores! You know, I had some computer training in grammar school, it was so basic, so rudimentary. Plus I never saw another computer until high school. So, if we don't start prioritizing as soon as these kids learn to read and understand basic math, we then need to get them on a computer or we are really going to put ourselves at a global disadvantage.

Mary Gatta: And of course what we are saying is that we cannot wait until an individual gets to the job to provide them with training. A career education system that addresses the entire pipeline needs to be incorporated within our education system.

Kevin McCabe: Nationally there needs to be a program that ties the workforce investment system to the middle school system. In New Jersey we have seen certain districts, in particular in the urban areas, where the dropout rate is at its highest after the ninth grade. We need to build better career systems within the public school system. Guidance counselors, teachers, and parents need to be aware of what are the growing jobs in the local economy and what are the pathways to get those jobs. In addition they all need to be aware of other noncollege career opportunities that are also afforded high school graduates, such as a developing a construction trade skill.

Mary Gatta: This again points to the importance of information on the market and a clear role for academia. We need to know what are the demand skills and the cutting edge ways to provide that training.

Kevin McCabe: It is imperative that government partners with as many stakeholders to begin to understand and formulate a clear working document that encompasses all the components of our economy. In developing the programs, government needs to be realistic to the daily issues that one faces, especially low-wage workers. I would contend that if you had an executive or mid-level manager who lost their job, they would be more inclined to successfully obtain another position because they have access to social networks, resources, and expertise. I think we take for granted the basic things that low-wage workers may not be able to do—develop a resume, participate in an interview, and other job readiness and life skills.

Mary Gatta: And there is maybe a role for the federal sector. The federal sector should provide resources for research that continually assess the demand skills. This data will help to better keep our training on target with the economy. It needs to be driven by good research about skills in demand. You do not have to look any farther than this alarming statistic. Sixty percent of the new jobs will require skills possessed by only 20 percent of the young people entering the labor market, unless we change the way that education and training systems operate (O'Leary, 2005).

Kevin McCabe: Our leadership in Washington needs to prioritize workforce development as a major issue as we did in New Jersey. The United States must be a high-wage and high-skill economy and must not compete at the lower end. Workers need to be trained continuously on the emerging technologies.

Mary Gatta: On the topic of the federal government, what role do you see them playing in helping low-wage workers secure self-sufficiency? WIA provides an opening to include low-wage workers in the federal employment and training dialogue, as it directs small amounts of training dollars to low-wage workers, and created the One-Stop System that is available to everyone. However, as we know, low-wage workers rarely take advantage of One-Stop Career Services because of the myriad of reasons we referenced earlier in the book. How do you suggest to engage the federal sector?

Kevin McCabe: I think it is the opposite of what you said. I think the federal government needs to engage the states and all the relevant partners. Similar to what we did in New Jersey, I believe that the federal government should call upon all Commissioners, Executive Staff, WIB Chairs, and WIB Directors for a workforce summit to develop a flexible working structure. And if there was such an opportunity, you would have to seek the input of the business coalitions (large and small businesses), community groups, educational entities, labor unions, academia and other key groups to develop a best practice for constructing a working flexible delivery system and mandate that state's utilize the suggestions. I believe that although WIA does provide for an outline, I think it needs to be taken a step further. As I noted throughout my discussion the bureaucratic structure is an obstacle. There needs to be a reappraisal of it. For example, although it is important, it just cannot be about performance numbers. I would contend that the long-term success of our economy should be treated as priority as you would any other crisis.

Mary Gatta: Are you suggesting that it is not a priority of the federal government?

Kevin McCabe: Not only do I do not believe that it is a priority of the current administration, I do not believe that it has been a core priority of any administration for the past two decades. By that I mean you cannot convince the American people and/or State Commissioners of Labor that it is a priority when training programs have been cut and hundreds of thousands of jobs have been exported oversees. Based on my conversations with CEOs in the pharmaceutical industry, after environmental issues the single most important element for them in deciding whether or not to maintain their business in the state is the assurance that there will be a qualified workforce for them to hire and train for their own specific purposes.

Mary Gatta: Clearly then not only must workforce development be a state priority, it needs to be a federal priority. For the past few years training programs have been characterized by this divestment of responsibility from the federal government to the states. Are you suggesting that this trend needs to be reversed?

Kevin McCabe: Not necessarily. If I were the Secretary of the United States Department of Labor I would look at, as I alluded to before, bringing together key partners to highlight best practices in the states. When New Jersey engaged in this process we did not just sit there and mandate changes for changes sake. We studied relevant research, we engaged in a two-way dialogue with the locals, and we studied what other states were doing. Let me just say this. I believe that if we did not make it a priority we would still be facing the same disjointed issues that we faced when we took office. Workforce training programs are seriously underfunded, and I maintain that workforce training as a whole has fallen off the nation's radar screen.

Mary Gatta: What then is the most important role than the federal government can play?

Kevin McCabe: Lead. Once again leading does not mean just mandating. I cannot stress that enough. The United States Department of Labor should be leading by first recognizing workforce development is a priority. Second, they must be willing to take the necessary steps to engage the states to understand the issues facing the economy and workers. Third, they must devise a comprehensive blueprint that will serve as a foundation, yet is flexible enough for each state to adapt to its own economic base. This is not an option Mary, it is a necessity for the long term security of this nation's economic viability and position in a rapidly changing global economy. Perhaps we can call this program "No Worker Left Behind" . . . except we would actually fund this program!

FINAL THOUGHTS

At no time in American history has the possession of skills and education been so necessary for individual's economic self-sufficiency and national competitiveness. Investing in the skills development of our current and future workforce is critical to our survival. As such throughout this book it has been demonstrated that workforce development is indeed economic development. This is achieved through both large and small steps. The online learning project for single working poor mothers that New Jersey piloted has now been institutionalized within its One-Stop Career system. In addition, several other states have begun similar pilot programs in order to provide training to groups of workers who previously did not have such access. It is important to note that the goal of such programs is not to replace classroom-based learning, but instead to provide alternatives for individuals who face barriers to traditional learning venues. Such programs empower individuals and provide them with the opportunities to improve their lives. Of course, a major point that needs to be stressed is that innovative programs do not just exist in a vacuum. We must make workforce development a federal and state priority throughout this country. In doing so we must invest the resources and the research to keep it cutting edge and tied to the economy market demands.

What workforce development really comes down to is improving individuals' lives. As I noted in the Preface to this book, I still recall the struggles that so many working poor single mothers faced working in the restaurants on the Jersey shore, as they tried to improve their lives. It is apparent that, from the perspective of fairness and economic necessity, workforce development must be transformed so that all workers have the opportunity to reach their full potential.

BIBLIOGRAPHY

Abramovitz, Mimi. 2001. "Everyone Is Still on Welfare: The Role of Redistribution in Social Policy." *Social Work* 46:297–302.

Abramovitz, Mimi. 2000. *Under Attack and Fighting Back: Women and Welfare in the United States.* New York: Monthly Review Press.

Abramovitz, Mimi. 1983. "Everyone Is on Welfare: The Role of Redistribution in Social Policy." *Social Work* 28:441–45.

Acs, Gregory and Pamela Loprest. 2004. "Leaving Welfare: Challenges in a New Economy." Kalamazoo, MI: W. E. Upjohn Institute for Employment Research.

Albeda, Randy and Chris Tilly. 1997. *Glass Ceilings and Bottomless Pits: Women's Work, Women's Poverty.* Boston, MA: South End Press.

American Association of University Women. 2001. *The Third Shift: Women Learning Online.* Washington, DC: AAUW Educational Foundation.

Appadurai, Arjun. 2002. "Grassroots, Globalization, and the Research Imagination." 271–84 in *The Anthropology of Politics.* Edited by Joan Vincent. Oxford, England: Blackwell Press.

Appelbaum, Eileen, Jared Bernstein, Janet Currie, Heidi Hartman, Lawrence Katz, Ann Markusen, Edward Montgomery, Steven Raphael, and Cecilia Rouse. 2004. "The Minimum Wage and Working Women." (http:www.cww.rutgers.edu).

Bae, Yupin, Susan Choy, Jennifer Sable Geddes, and Thomas Snyder. 2000. *Trends in Educational Equity of Girls and Women.* Washington, DC: National Center for Education Statistics.

Bartik, Timothy. 2001. *Jobs for the Poor: Can Labor Demand Policies Help?* New York: Russell Sage Foundation.

Bernhardt, Annette, Martina Morrus, Mark Handcock, and Marc Scott. 2001. *Divergent Paths: Economic Mobility in the New American Labor Market.* New York: Russell Sage Foundation.

Bielby, William and James Baron. 1986. "Men and Women at Work: Sex Segregation and Statistical Discrimination." *American Journal of Sociology* 91:759–99.

Bloomfield, Jacqueline. 2001. "Meeting the Challenges of Distance Learning."
Australian Nursing Journal 6:40.

Bok, Marcia. 2004. "Education and Training for Low-Income Women: An Elusive
Goal." *Affilia* 19:39–52.

Boris, Eileen. 1998. "When Work Is Slavery." 36–56 in *Whose Welfare?* Edited by
Gwendolyn Mink. Ithaca, NY: Cornell University Press.

Boushey, Heather, Chauna Brocht, Bethney Gundersen, and Jared Bernstein.
2001. "Hardships in America: The Real Story of Working Families." Washington
DC: Economic Policy Institute.

Browne, Irene and Joya Misra. 2003. "The Intersection of Gender and Race in the
Labor Market." *Annual Review of Sociology* 29:487–513.

Bruner and Bennett. 1998. "Technology Perceptions by Gender." *Education Digest*
63:56–59.

Buck, Maria. 2002. "Charting New Territory: Early Implementation of WIA." *Pub-
lic/Private Ventures*. (http://www.ppv.org).

Burawoy, Michael. 2004. "Public Sociologies: Contradictions, Dilemma, and Possi-
bilities." *Social Forces* 52:1603–18.

Carnevale, Anthony. 1999. "Beyond Consensus: Much Ado about Job Training."
Brookings Review 17:40–43.

Capps, Randy, Michael Fox, Jeffrey Passel, Jason Ost, and Dan Perez-Lopez. 2003.
"A Profile of the Low-Wage Immigrant Workforce." Washington, DC: The
Urban Institute.

Carnevale, Anthony and Donna Descrochus. 1999. "Getting Down to Business:
Matching Welfare Recipients Skills to Jobs That Train." Princeton, NJ: Educational Testing Service.

Cernea, Michael. 1993/1994. "Social Science Research and the Crafting of Policy
on Population Resettlement." *Knowledge and Policy* 6(3/4):176–201.

Chapman, Jeff and Jared Bernstein. 2003. "Falling through the Safety Net: Low-
Income Mothers in the Jobless Recovery." Washington DC: Economic Policy
Institute Brief.

Chicago Jobs Council. 2003. "Improving our Response to Work Needs: Recommendations for Reauthorization of the Workforce Investment Act of 1998." Chicago, IL: Chicago Jobs Council.

Collins, Patricia Hill. 1999. *Black Feminist Thought: Knowledge, Consciousness,
and the Politics of Empowerment.* 2nd Edition. London: HarperCollins.

Conway, Maureen and Lily Zandiapour. 2002. "Industry-Based Employment Programs: Implications for Welfare Reauthorization and Key Survey Findings."
Washington, DC: The Aspen Institute.

Corcoran, Mary, Sandra Danziger, Ariel Kalil, and Kristen Seifeldt. 2000. "How
Welfare Reform Is Affecting Women's Work." *Annual Review of Sociology*
26:241–69.

Crittenden, Anne. 2001. *The Price of Motherhood: Why the Most Important Job in the World Is Still the Least Valued.* New York: Owl Books.

D'Amico, Ronald and Jeffrey Salzman. 2004. "Implementation Issues in Delivering Training Services to Adults Under WIA." 101–34 in *Job Training Policy in the United States.* Edited by Christopher O'Leary, Robert Straits, and Stephen Wandner. Kalamazoo, MI: W. E. Upjohn Institute for Employment Research.

Dill, Bonnie Thornton, Avis Jones-DeWeever, and Sanford Schram. 2004. "Racial, Ethnic, and Gender Disparities in Access to Jobs, Education, and Training Under Welfare Reform." College Park, MD: Consortium on Race, Gender, and Ethnicity.

Djoudi, Mahieddine and Saad Harous. 2001. "Simplifying the Learning Process Over the Internet." *T H E Journal* 29:50–55.

Edin, Kathyrn and Laura Lein. 1997. *Making Ends Meet: How Single Mothers Survive Welfare and Low-Wage Work.* New York: Russell Sage Foundation.

Ehrenreich, Barbara. 2001. *Nickel and Dimed: On (Not) Getting By in America.* New York: Metropolitan/Owl Books.

Folbe, Nancy. 2001. *The Invisible Heart: Economics and Family Values.* New York: The New Press.

Fox-Piven, Frances. 1999. "Welfare and Work." 83–99 in *Whose Welfare?* Edited by Gwendolyn Mink. Ithaca, NY: Cornell University Press.

Fox-Piven, Frances and Richard Cloward. 1993. *Regulating the Poor: The Function of Public Welfare.* 2nd Edition. New York: Vintage Books.

Freeman, Jennifer and Judith Combes Taylor. 2002. "Beyond Welfare-to-Work: Helping Low-Income Workers Maintain Their Jobs and Advance in the Workforce. Paper #1: Demand-Led Retention." Paper prepared for the United States Department of Labor Future @ Work Follow-Up Project: Working Seminar on Retention Strategies. Boston, MA.

Furst-Bowe, Julie. 2001. "Identifying the Needs of Adult Women in Distance Learning Programs." University of Wisconsin-Stout, Unpublished Paper.

Gans, Sheldon and Gerald Horton. 1975. *Integration of Human Services: The State and Municipal Levels.* New York: Praeger Publishers.

Ganzglass, Evelyn, Martin Jensen, Neil Ridley, Martin Simon, and Chris Thompson. 2001. "Transforming State Workforce Development Systems: Case Studies of Five Leading States." Washington, DC: National Governor's Association.

Gatta, Mary and Kevin P. McCabe. 2005. *Not Just Getting By: Implementing Innovative Thinking in Government and Workforce Development.* Lanham, MA: Lexington Press.

Gatta, Mary and Patricia A. Roos. 2004. "Balancing Without a Net in Academia: Integrating Family and Work Lives." *Equal Opportunities International* 23:124–42.

Gault, Barbara. 2002. "Utilizing the Workforce Investment Act Programs and TANF to Provide Education and Training Opportunities to Reduce Poverty

Among Low-Income Women." Testimony before the United States House Education and Workforce Committee.

Gervey, Robert, Ni Gao, and Dennis Rizzo. 2004. "Gloucester County One-Stop Project: Baseline Level of Access and Satisfaction of One-Stop Center Customers with Disabilities." *Journal of Vocational Rehabilitation* 21:103–15.

Gilbert, Melissa. 1998. "Race, Space, and Power: The Survival Strategies of Working Poor Women." *Annals of the Association of American Geographers* 88:595–621.

Glenn, Evelyn Nakano. 1999. "The Social Construction and Institutionalization of Gender and Race: An Integrative Framework." 3–43 in *Revisioning Gender.* Edited by Myra Max Ferree, Judith Lorber, and Beth Hess. Thousand Oaks, CA: Sage Publications.

Grubb, W. Norton. 1999. "From Isolation to Integration: Occupational Education and the Emerging Systems of Workforce Development." Berkley, CA: National Center for Research in Vocational Education.

Hanson, Susan and Geraldine Pratt. 1995. *Gender, Work, and Space.* New York: Routledge Press.

Hanson, Susan and Ibipo Johnston. 1985. "Gender Differences in Worktrip Length: Explanations and Implications." *Urban Geography* 9:180–202.

Harrington, Paul and Andrew Sum. 2002. "Workforce Development Challenges for the Twenty-first Century." A Report of the United States Conference of Mayors. Northeastern University, Boston, MA.

Harrison, Bennett and Marcus Weiss. 1998. *Workforce Development Networks: Community Based Organizations and Regional Alliances.* Thousand Oaks, CA: Sage Publications.

Hayes, Sharon. 2003. *Flat Broke with Children: Women in the Age of Welfare Reform.* London: Oxford University Press.

Hochschild, Arlie Russell. (1989) 2003. *The Second Shift.* New York: Penguin Books.

Hochschild, Arlie Russell.1983. *The Managed Heart: Commercialization of Human Feeling.* Berkeley, CA: University of California Press.

hooks, bell. 1989. *Talking Back: Thinking Feminist, Thinking Black.* Boston, MA: South End Press.

Iceland, John and David Rebar. 2001. "Measuring the Impact of Childcare Expenses on Poverty." Paper presented at the 2001 Population Association of America Meetings, Washington DC.

Institute for Women's Policy Research. 2001. *Working First, But Working Poor: The Need for Education and Skills Training Following Welfare.* Washington, DC: IWPR.

Institute for Women's Policy Research. 2002. "Welfare, Poverty, and Marriage: What Does the Research Say?" Washington DC: IWPR Newsletter.

Jacobs, Ronald. 2002. "Understanding Workforce Development: Definition, Conceptual Boundaries, and Future Perspectives." Paper presented at the International Conference on Technical and Vocational Education and Training, Winnipeg, Manitoba.

Jacobs, Ronald. 2000. "Managing Employee Competence and Human Intelligence in Global Organizations." 65–71 in *Philosophy of Human Resource Development*. Edited by Frank-Jurgen Richter. San Francisco, CA: Berrett-Koehler Publishers.

Johnson, Jennifer. 2002. *Getting By on the Minimum: The Lives of Working Class Women*. New York: Routledge Press.

Karier, Thomas. 1998. "Welfare Graduates: College and Financial Independence." New York: The Levy Economics Institute.

Kessler-Harris, Alice. 2001. *In Pursuit of Equity: Women, Men, and the Quest for Economic Citizenship in the Twentieth Century*. New York: Oxford University Press.

Kessler-Harris, Alice. 1982. *Out to Work: A History of Wage Earning Women in the United States*. London: Oxford University Press.

Kittay, Eva. 1998. "Welfare, Dependency, and a Public Ethic of Care." 189–214 in *Whose Welfare?* Edited by Gwendolyn Mink. Ithaca, NY: Cornell University Press.

Kossek, Ellen Ernst, Melissa Huber-Yoder, Domini Castellino, and Jacqueline Lerner. 1997. "The Working Poor: Locked Out of Careers and the Organizational Mainstream." *Academy of Management Executive* 11:76–92.

Lafer, Gordon. 2004. *The Job Training Charade*. Ithaca, NY: Cornell University Press.

Lerman, Robert and Felicity Skidmore. 1999. "Helping Low-Wage Workers: Policies for the Future." Presentation at the Urban Institute Conference, Washington, DC.

Levenson, Alec, Elaine Reardon, and Stefanie Schmidt. 1999. "Welfare, Jobs, and Basic Skills: The Employment Prospects of Welfare Recipients in the Most Populous U.S. Counties." NCSALL Reports #10B. National Center for the Study of Adult Learning and Literacy, Boston, MA.

Levitan, Mark and Robin Gluck. 2004. *Mother's Work: Single Mothers Employment, Earnings, and Poverty in the Age of Welfare Reform*. New York: Community Service Society.

Luker, Kristin. 1985. *Abortion and the Politics of Motherhood*. Berkeley: University of California Press.

Lynch, Lisa and Sandra Black. 1995. "Beyond the Incidence of Training: Evidence from the National Employer Survey." Working Paper No. 5231, National Bureau of Economic Research.

Maine Equal Justice Partners. 2001. "Parents as Scholars Program." Augusta, ME.

Marini, Margaret. 1989. "Sex Differences in Earnings in the United States." *Annual Review of Sociology* 62:343–80.

Mars, Gerald and Michael Nicod. 1984. *The World of Waiters*. London, England: Allen and Unwin.

Martison, Karin. 1999. "Literature Review on Service Coordination and Integration in the Welfare and Workforce Development Systems." Publication of the Urban Institute. Washington, DC: Urban Institute Press.

Massing, Michael. 2002. "Ending Poverty as We Know It." 21–37 in *Making Work Pay: Life after Welfare*. Edited by Robert Kuttner. New York: The New Press.

Mazzella, Beth. 2000. "Collaboration, Challenge, Risk, and Reward. The Dynamics of Working Together: A Review of the Barriers and Strategies Shaping Inter-agency Collaboration." Paper presented at the fifth Annual Aging and Mental Retardation Conference, Boston, MA.

McCall, Leslie. 2001. *Complex Inequality: Gender, Class, and Race in a Restructuring Economy*. New York: Routledge Press.

Metzel, Deborah, Susan Foley, and John Butterworth. 2002. "From Paper to Action: State Level Inter-agency Agreements for Supported Employment of People with Disabilities." Boston, MA: Institute for Community Inclusion.

Miller, Jennifer, Frieda Molina, Lisa Grossman, and Susan Golonka. 2004. "Building Bridges to Self-Sufficiency: Improving Services for Low-Income Working Families." New York: MDRC.

Mills, C. Wright. 1959. *The Sociological Imagination*. New York: Oxford University Press.

Mink, Gwendolyn and Rickie Solinger. 2003. *Welfare: A Documentary History of Policy and Politics*. New York: New York University Press.

Mink, Gwendolyn. 1999. *Whose Welfare?* Ithaca, NY: Cornell University Press.

Mink, Gwendolyn. 1993. "Welfare, Women, and Race." *American Quarterly* 45:671–82.

National Governor's Association. 2002. "A Governor's Guide to Creating a twenty-first Century Workforce." Washington, DC: National Governor's Association.

Negrey, Cynthia, Annisah Um'rani, Stacie Golin, and Barbara Gault. 2000. "Job Training Under Welfare Reform: Opportunities for and Obstacles to Economic Self-Sufficiency among Low-Income Women." *Georgetown Journal on Poverty, Law, and Policy* 7:347–62.

New Jersey State Employment and Training Commission. 2001. "New Jersey in Transition: The Crisis of the Workforce." Trenton, NJ: SETC.

Nielsen, Francios. 2004. "The Vacant 'We': Remarks on Public Sociology." *Social Forces* 82:1619–27.

Noyes, Jennifer and Shawn Smith. 2004. "Connecting the Dots: Can the United States Integrate Welfare Reform and Workforce Development?" Indianapolis, IN: Hudson Institute.

O'Connor, Alice. 2000. "Poverty Research and Policy for the Post-Welfare Era." *Annual Review of Sociology* 26:547–62.

O'Neill, June and M. Anne Hill. 2002. "Gaining Ground: Women, Welfare Reform and Work." Dallas, TX: NCPA Policy Report.

Petersen, Trond and Laurie A. Morgan. 1995. "Separate and Unequal: Occupation-Establishment Sex Segregation and the Gender Wage Gap." *American Journal of Sociology* 101:329–65.

Pierce, Diana and Jennifer Brooks. 2002. "The Real Cost of Living: The Self-Sufficiency Standard for New Jersey." Edison, NJ: Legal Services of New Jersey Poverty Research Institute.

Reich, Robert. 2002. "Working Principles: From Ending Welfare Reform to Rewarding Work." vii–xvii in *Making Work Pay: Life After Welfare*. Edited by Robert Kuttner. New York: The New Press.

Relave, Nanette. 2000. "Collaboration between the Welfare and Workforce Development Systems." A Publication of the Welfare Information Network Issue Notes. (http://www.financeprojectinfo.org/win/).

Reskin, Barbara and Irene Padavic. 2002. *Women and Men at Work*. Second Edition. Thousand Oaks, CA: Pine Forge Press.

Reskin, Barbara and Irene Padavic. 1994. *Women and Men at Work*. Thousand Oaks, CA: Pine Forge Press.

Rich, Adrienne. 1986. *Of Woman Born: Motherhood as Experience and Institution*. New York: W. W. Norton and Company.

Roberts, Dorothy. 1999. "Welfare's Ban on Poor Motherhood." 152–70 in *Whose Welfare?* Edited by Gwendolyn Mink. Ithaca, NY: Cornell University Press.

Roche, Ann. 2000. "What Is This Thing Called Workforce Development?" Adelaida, South Australia: National Centre for Education and Training on Addiction.

Roos, Patricia and Mary L. Gatta. 1999. "The Gender Gap in Earnings." 95–123 in *The Handbook of Gender and Work*. Edited by Gary Powell. Thousand Oaks, CA: Sage Publications.

Schulman, Beth. 2003. *The Betrayal of Work: How Low-Wage Jobs Fail 30 Million Americans*. New York: The New Press.

Sklar, Holly, Laryssa Mykta, and Susan Wefald. 2001. *Raise the Floor: Wages and Policies that Work for All of Us*. New York: Ms. Foundation for Women.

Solinger, Rickie. 1998. "Dependency and Choice: The Two Faces of Eve." 7–36 in *Whose Welfare?* Edited by Gwendolyn Mink. Ithaca, NY: Cornell University Press.

Strawn, Julie and Robert Eichols. 1999. "Welfare to Work Programs: The Critical Role of Skills." Washington, DC: Center for Law and Social Policy.

Timmons, Jaimie Ciulla, Sheila Lynch Fesko, and Allison Cohen. 2004. "Merging Cultural Differences and Professional Identities: Strategies for Maximizing Collaborative Efforts during the Implementation of the Workforce Investment Act." *Journal of Rehabilitation* 70:19–27.

United States Department of Labor, Bureau of Labor Statistics. 2004. "A Profile of the Working Poor." Washington, DC.

United States Department of Labor, Bureau of Labor Statistics, 2004. "Women in the Labor Force: A Databook." Washington, DC.

Van Horn, Carl and Herbert Schaffner. 2003. "Winning the Workforce Challenge: A Report on New Jersey's Knowledge Economy." New Brunswick, NJ: John J. Heldrich Center for Workforce Development.

Waldron, Tom, Brandon Roberts, and Andrew Reamer. 2004. "Working Hard, Falling Short." Chevy Chase, MD: Working Poor Families Project.

Weir, Margaret. 1992. *Politics and Jobs: The Boundaries of Employment Policy in the United States.* Princeton, NJ: Princeton University Press.

Wider Opportunities for Women. 2003. "Reauthorizing the Workforce Investment Act: More Can Be Done to Expand the Economic Opportunities for Women and Families." Proceedings from United States Congressional Briefing. Washington, DC.

Williams, Joan. 2000. *Unbending Gender: Why Family and Work Conflict and What to Do about It.* New York: Oxford University Press.

Worthen, Helen. 2004. "The Workforce Investment Act and the Labor Movement." 76–89 in *Welfare, Working Poor, and Labor.* Edited by Louise Simmons. Armonk, NY: M. E. Sharpe.

INDEX

Temporary Aid to Need Families, 43, 55
third shift, 15–16
Tilly, Charles, 26, 45, 57–58, 62
tips as income, 23–24
triple whammy, 62

United States Commission on Civil
    Rights, 54
United States Conference of Mayors, 7
United States Department of Labor,
    xviii
United States Department of Labor,
    Employment and Training Adminis-
    tration, xviii
United States Department of Labor,
    Women's Bureau, xviii
Upjohn Institute, 27
Urban Institute, 27
USDOL. *See* United States Depart-
    ment of Labor

wage gap, 24, 34
Wefald, Susan, 57
welfare: corporate, 44; dependency on,
    40–46; deservingness of, 40, 40–52;
    fiscal, 44; gender and, 40–46; history
    of, 46–56; marriage promotion and,
    46; means tested v. non-means
    tested, 44; occupational, 44; popular
    portrayal of, 43, 52; race/ethnicity
    and, 40–46; single mothers and,
    46–52; social justice and, 45; value of
    women and, 45
welfare reform, 27; gender ideology
    and, 48, 52–56; increased work par-
    ticipation and, 39; low-wage work
    and, 52–56; motherhood ideology
    and, 48–52, 53–55; performance
    measures of, 39–40; racial ideology
    and, 48, 52–56; southern states, 54
WIA. *See* Workforce Investment Act
WIB. *See* Workforce Investment Board

Wider Opportunities for Women, 13
work/family/education integration, xvi,
    15–16, 19, 57–58, 73–75
Workfirst, 11–12, 23, 35, 55, 57
workforce development system: defini-
    tion of, 5–8, 112; demand skills and,
    6, 33, 34, 86, 112; economic develop-
    ment, 6, 13, 31–33, 86, 111, 113–
    114; employers and, 5, 33; federal
    government role, 115–117; flexibility
    and, xiv, 5–7, 13, 76–77, 83, 98–99,
    106, 111–114; K-12 education sys-
    tem and, 87–89, 114–115; long-term
    results of, 6–7; national priority of,
    111, 114–117; reconceptualization
    of, xvi, 2, 20–21, 35–36; state priority
    of, 111, 115–117; technology and,
    113–114
Workforce Investment Act, 4, 34–35,
    61, 89–90, 115; collaborations,
    11–12; definition of, 8–10; flexibility
    and, 13; goals of, 8; JTPA as com-
    pared to, 8–9; performance mea-
    sures of, 35; problems with, 12–13,
    35; training services, 9
Workforce Investment Board, 64–65,
    89–90, 92–94; definition of, 10
Working Families Project, 32
working poor: definition of, 1, 21–23;
    demographics of, 24, 39–40; gender
    and, 21; hardship measures of, 27;
    healthcare access and, 26; income of,
    22, 23–24; participation in job train-
    ing programs, 20–21; race/ethnicity
    and, 21, 22; single mothers as part of,
    21–22; training job policies and,
    20–21
Works Progress Administration, 33
WOW. *See* Wider Opportunities for
    Women
WPA. *See* Works Progress Administra-
    tion

ABOUT THE AUTHORS

Dr. Mary L. Gatta is Director of Workforce Policy and Research at the Center for Women and Work at Rutgers University. She holds a Ph.D. in Sociology from Rutgers University, an M.A. in Sociology from Rutgers University, and a B.A. in Social Science from Providence College.

Dr. Gatta currently directs the Sloan Center on Innovative Training and Workforce Development. This center provides technical assistance and resources to states to scale up a New Jersey pilot project of online learning for low-wage workers throughout the country. In addition, she works collaboratively with the labor unions, state governments, and other workforce entities to help craft programs for low-wage workers.

Her book, *Juggling Food and Feelings: Emotional Balance in the Workplace*, was released from Lexington Press in 2002. In addition to books, she has published numerous scholarly articles and public policy papers on topics including gender equity in academia, workforce development policies for low-wage workers, and occupational sex segregation.

Kevin P. McCabe is currently the Director of Special Projects at the New Jersey Regional Council of Carpenters. Prior to that appointment he served New Jersey as Deputy Commissioner and then Commissioner of the Department of Labor and Workforce Development. In that position he led an ambitious effort to make it easier for both workers and employers to navigate the job training, counseling, and benefits the Department provides. In addition, McCabe oversaw all job training and workforce development programs, business services, labor market information, unemployment insurance, disability services, and enforcement of the state's labor standards and safety rules.

Prior to joining the Department of Labor, McCabe served in the Office of the Mayor of Woodbridge Township, beginning in 1992. He served in several administrative capacities, including chief of staff.

Mr. McCabe holds an M.A in Public Administration from Rutgers University and a B.A. in Political Science from Kean University.